The Knitting Encyclopedia

D0573641

Lo

WITHDRAWN

The Knitting Encyclopedia

A Comprehensive Guide For All Knitters

CLAIRE MONTGOMERIE

3 1336 08977 1456

St. Martin's Griffin

New York

THE KNITTING ENCYCLOPEDIA.
Copyright © 2012 by Quintet. All rights
reserved.
For information, address St. Martin's Press,
175 Fifth Avenue, New York, N.Y. 10010.

www.stmartins.com

First U.S. Edition: March 2012

A Quintet Book.
Copyright © 2012 Quintet Publishing Limited.
All rights reserved.

QTT.KTD

The written instructions, photographs,
designs, patterns, and projects in this volume
are intended for personal use of the reader
and may be reproduced for that purpose only.

Library of Congress Cataloging-in-Publication
Data available upon request

This book was deigned and produced by
Quintet Publishing Limited, 6 Blundell Street,
London, N7 9BH, UK

QTT.KTD

Project Editor: Asha Savjani
Editorial Assistant: Sarah Quinlan
Designer: Bonnie Bryan
Photographer: David Murphy
Illustrator: Bernard Chau
Art Director: Michael Charles
Managing Editor: Donna Gregory
Publisher: Mark Searle

ISBN: 978–0–312–64016–3

First U.S. Edition: 2012

Printed in China

10 9 8 7 6 5 4 3 2 1

Contents

Projects

Introduction

Knitting is an ancient craft, using techniques that have been handed down from generation to generation over the last few millennia. It is extremely difficult to say exactly when and by whom the art of knitting was invented, but there is evidence to suggest that knitted fabrics have been part of civilization for thousands of years.

The word "knitting" comes from an Old English word meaning "a knot," and basic techniques have changed little over the centuries. The early knitters were the men of tribes, and they were very skilled at their craft. As these people kept straggling herds of sheep and goats there was no shortage of material for them to knit with. The women gathered wool from the animals and spun it into yarn for the men, who would sit for hours, tending the flocks and knitting. The articles they produced were simple scarves, robes, and socks to wear with sandals.

Ancient knitting

Very few examples of really early knitting are still in existence, but a pair of red sandal socks, pre-Christian in origin, does still survive. They are beautifully made, with expertly turned heels. It is interesting to note that the stitches have been carefully divided for the big toe, so that the socks were comfortable to wear with sandals.

Between AD1000 and 1200, little round knitted caps known as "Coptic caps" were being made in Egypt. The caps were worn by traveling monks and missionaries, and it is possible that these men carried the knowledge of knitting with them out of Egypt. Craftsmen in Spain, then in Italy and France, and eventually in England and the New World, were fascinated by this new kind of fabric weaving. Knowledge of the craft quickly spread, with each nation adding its own ideas and patterns. By the Middle Ages knitting was a common craft form all over Europe.

Around the sixteenth century, advances in metalworking technology meant that fine-gauge knitting needles were becoming easier to produce. Knitting became a thriving trade, with men training for up to six years to become a Master Guild knitter.

Elizabeth I of England had a passion for silk stockings with lace patterns knitted to an incredibly fine gauge. During her reign, a more primitive style of knitting was commonly used by small farming communities, who supplemented their incomes by producing and selling a pair of stockings per family member weekly. By the seventeenth century, hand knitting was a trade usually practiced only by the lower classes.

Knitted jacket. Hand knit in silk silver
gilt wrapped silk lined with linen.
England or Italy, AD 1625–1650.

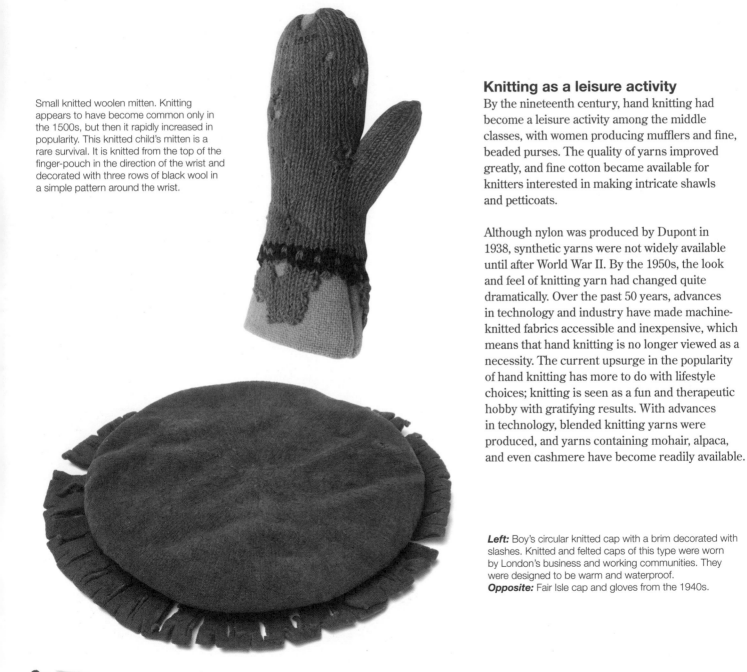

Small knitted woolen mitten. Knitting appears to have become common only in the 1500s, but then it rapidly increased in popularity. This knitted child's mitten is a rare survival. It is knitted from the top of the finger-pouch in the direction of the wrist and decorated with three rows of black wool in a simple pattern around the wrist.

Knitting as a leisure activity

By the nineteenth century, hand knitting had become a leisure activity among the middle classes, with women producing mufflers and fine, beaded purses. The quality of yarns improved greatly, and fine cotton became available for knitters interested in making intricate shawls and petticoats.

Although nylon was produced by Dupont in 1938, synthetic yarns were not widely available until after World War II. By the 1950s, the look and feel of knitting yarn had changed quite dramatically. Over the past 50 years, advances in technology and industry have made machine-knitted fabrics accessible and inexpensive, which means that hand knitting is no longer viewed as a necessity. The current upsurge in the popularity of hand knitting has more to do with lifestyle choices; knitting is seen as a fun and therapeutic hobby with gratifying results. With advances in technology, blended knitting yarns were produced, and yarns containing mohair, alpaca, and even cashmere have become readily available.

Left: Boy's circular knitted cap with a brim decorated with slashes. Knitted and felted caps of this type were worn by London's business and working communities. They were designed to be warm and waterproof.
Opposite: Fair Isle cap and gloves from the 1940s.

Yarns and fibers

Since making cloth began, a wide variety of fibers have been used to spin yarn. In fact, some "newfangled" yarns are not as modern as you might think. Nettles, for example, have been used in clothing for thousands of years. The plant only lost favor because of the comparative ease of harvesting cotton. Nettles made a resurrection at the start of the twentieth century, when they were used in German military uniforms because the war reduced the availability of cotton and wool.

Animal, vegetable, and mineral

The twenty-first-century resurgence of natural fibers is partially due to concerns about the manufacturing processes used to make synthetic yarns. Nonetheless, natural and synthetic fibers have advantages and disadvantages, and both can be useful in experimental knitting.

Vegetable fibers mostly comprise cellulose, and they come from various parts of the plant. An excellent example is cotton, which is harvested from seed. Hemp, soybean, and banana are collected from around the skin of the stem; bamboo and linen are gathered from the stalk.

Fibers can also be obtained from fruits, such as coconut, and its leaves, which is the case with sisal. Paper and bark yarns are derived from cellulose fibers, too.

Animal fibers contain proteins, and usually come from animal hair, such as wool, angora, cashmere, llama, and even dog. From the silkworms' cocoons comes silk, another prominent animal fiber.

Mineral fibers include metals and fiberglass, which are occasionally used as embellishments.

Animal fibers are natural fibers that consist largely of proteins. Common instances include silk, hair/fur (including wool) and feathers.

The housewife's dream?

Synthetic fibers were created to replicate or improve on the qualities of natural fibers. This class includes nylon, polyester, and acrylic.

Manmade fibers such as rayon or viscose are manufactured but not completely synthetic, because they are produced from cellulose fibers. Rayon was developed in the mid-nineteenth century as an artificial silk. Scientists have always been intrigued by the strength of silk, and some have researched the production of an artificial spider-silk fiber.

Acrylic was developed as a synthetic wool because it is popular for knitting, looks like wool, is lightweight, resilient, moth resistant, and is incredibly colorfast. However, it pills, or bobbles, easily, is not as insulating as wool, and is not always as soft.

These new fabrics and fibers aimed to be the answer to every housewife's dream: incredibly creaseproof, simple to maintain, easily dyed, and cheap to produce. However, the wearing qualities didn't always live up to the hype.

Acrylic has recently been used in clothing as a less expensive alternative to cashmere, due to the similar feeling of the materials.

Metallic rayon thread is manufactured from regenerated cellulose fiber.

The best of both worlds

Perhaps the answer to the perfect yarn is to combine fibers. Some of the most durable and comfortable yarns available today are a mixture of natural and synthetic fibers.

Merino wool socks, for example, are luxurious, but they are likely to wear out. Therefore, most sock yarns have a little nylon or another synthetic fiber added to the natural yarn to increase durability. Many yarns are now treated or mixed with synthetics, so they can be machine washed without risk of felting. These synthetic fibers are all fabulous, but natural yarns still have their uses. There is no need to create water-repellent, insulating, and light fibers when wool has all of these qualities. When wool is spun and knitted properly, it is naturally unsurpassed in all of these qualities. Most natural fibers tend to have fantastic drape, which is an added benefit to their naturally practical qualities, such as the strength

of silk. Synthetic yarns can find excellent use in fancy yarns to create unusual textures, such as eyelash fringing and also strange, knobbly yarns that do not shed hair or fiber and can be good for allergy sufferers.

A fiber's qualities often dictate how it is used. Cotton yarn is usually spun with a smooth finish and it is durable, making it the traditional and best choice for crochet. It is available in a range of weights and colors, including many fabulous summer shades—it is often used as a summer-weight alternative to wool. Cotton usually has a matte finish. However, if you prefer your yarn with a shine and extra strength, choose mercerized cotton. Organic cotton is a sustainable alternative to plants grown with fertilizers and chemicals. And it is easy to reprocess—there are many varieties of recycled cotton yarn available.

Yarns galore

There are many varieties of wool and mohair, derived from sheep and goats. The qualities vary from merino, to cashmere, to kid mohair—but all of them are extremely warm, and usually soft and with a matte finish.

Silk is incredibly strong, with a mesmerizing sheen and drape that adds to its luxury. This is a great summer choice and fabulous when mixed with matte yarns.

Synthetic yarns can have a multitude of qualities, thicknesses, and textures. When they are combined with natural yarns, they can help garments hold their shape when worn and washed.

Staples and filaments

To understand more about how a yarn is constructed, you must know about the fibers mainly used in this process.

First, there are staple fibers, which are of a limited, usually very short length. These can be as small as ⅜ in (1 cm) long. In order to form a yarn with these fibers, they have to be spun or twisted together into longer lengths. The spinning process can form many different textures.

The other type of fibers are filaments, which are longer fibers that can be measured in yards or meters or, if manmade, even in miles. Examples of a natural filament include silk fibers, which gain smoothness from the length of the filament.

Tussah silk from wild silk worms

Merino sheep wool fibers

Tencel or lyocell fibers made from cellulose

Soya bean protein fibers

Green untreated cotton fibers

Black alpaca mixed with silk fibers

Flax or linen fibers

Milk protein fiber from casein

Spinning yarns

All of the fibers mentioned so far can be spun into many types of yarn. They may be one long, smooth plied length, or varied to create fancy yarns, such as bouclé, gimp, slub, eyelash, and chenille.

The yarn does not always need to be spun, though. It can be used in its essential form, as roving, or the fiber can be knitted into a tape yarn or woven into a ribbon yarn. All of these yarns have particular qualities that can be incorporated into your knitting to inspire and create themes. A ribbon yarn may evoke draping fabric or tumbling water. A roving yarn retains the look of the fleece it was carded from, making fluffy sheeplike clouds in knitted fabrics. And the drama of eyelash yarn, depending on its lengths, can represent the fringing, curling tendrils of plant stamens or lush coverings of moss.

All of these yarns are classified by weight, thickness, or ply, so it is easy for the knitter to substitute yarns, select the correct needles, and judge the right gauge.

Traditional hand spinning is the ancient textile art of twisting fibers together (plant, animal, or synthetic) to create yarn.

The projects in this book use a range of yarns, selected for the variety of their thicknesses and fibers. Easier projects, aimed at beginners, tend to make use of more traditional yarns which have been specially chosen to suit the project. For example, Fair Isle projects use colors that complement the pattern, projects using cable stitch must have clearly defined stitches, and any felting must be done with pure wool.

There is a detailed summary of these classifications on pages 22–23. There is also a list of the types of yarns on pages 16–21 that will make it easy to choose alternative yarns for the patterns. The yarn list can also be used as a guide when you choose yarns for your own projects.

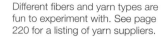

Different fibers and yarn types are fun to experiment with. See page 220 for a listing of yarn suppliers.

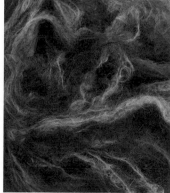

Using a range of yarn thicknesses and textures allows you to vary your projects without changing stitch.

Types of yarn

There are so many types of yarn available today that knitters are spoiled for choice. Here are the standard types you might come across.

Single yarn

The simplest strand of fiber—a single yarn—is a mass of fibers bonded into one yarn by spinning or twisting. A yarn can be spun or plied in many ways to create smooth or textured yarns.

Woolen yarn

Woolen yarn is not necessarily a yarn made from wool fibers, though of course, wool can be used. It is just the term used to describe short staple fibers of varying lengths that are spun to produce an airy, fluffy, warm yarn that is elastic.

Worsted yarn

A worsted yarn is formed from longer staple fibers, similar in length, that have been combed to ensure that the staples are parallel, creating an extra-smooth yarn when spun. The resulting yarn is strong and inelastic. It is extremely useful to know the difference between these two types of yarn when deciding on the fiber to use for a garment, because the woolen yarn will be naturally warmer for cold winter days, and the worsted yarn will produce a cooler garment for warm summer evenings.

Roving

Roving is an unspun mass of fibers, drawn or rubbed into a single strand, so that they are parallel to each other. This is usually the state of carded fibers, the stage prior to spinning worsted yarns. This is not necessarily a yarn, but it can be knitted as one, providing a super-bulky effect.

Plied yarn

A plied yarn is made by twisting together two or more single yarns in one direction. This direction can either be to the left, which is called "s" (counterclockwise) twist, or to the right, which is called "z" (clockwise) twist. Plying yarns makes them stronger and more regimented.

Blended yarn

Blended yarn comprises more than one type of fiber.

Double and twist yarn

This two-color yarn is spun by twisting together yarns of different colors to form a spiral effect.

Marl or mottled yarn

This is a process in which two singles of differing solid colors, or dyed with differing techniques, are doubled and spun into a single yarn.

Novelty or fancy yarn

Yarns that have irregularities placed into them during the spinning process are described as "novelty" or "fancy."

Slub

A slub is produced by adding the yarn to be spun at differing speeds so that the resulting yarn varies in thickness. A slub can also be added to the yarn being spun by inserting "bumps" of fiber from a separate source.

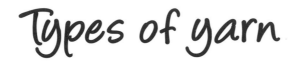

Yarn is spun by twisting fibers together. Traditionally this was done by hand using a spindle and distaff.

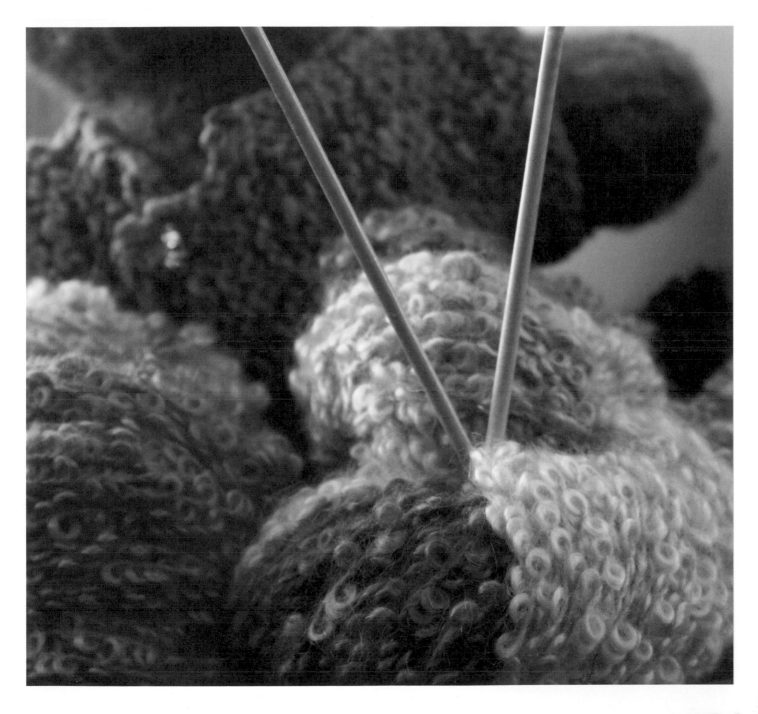

A swatch made from bouclé shows this yarn's interesting color and texture potential.

Loops

When two or more threads are spun together, the gauge each yarn is held at can contribute to the ultimate texture of the yarn. A looped yarn consists of two singles held at different gauges when spun so that the looser yarn buckles up and twists into clearly defined circular loops at regular intervals along the final yarn.

Within this group are bouclé yarns, which are formed in the same way but have smaller full-circle or semicircular loops positioned at irregular intervals along the length of yarn.

A gimp yarn is created by binding an irregular single with a regular single at differing gauges to create graduating, semicircular loops and bumps along the yarn.

Coils, worms, or beehives

A coiled yarn is also called a worm or beehive, due to its texture of satisfyingly fat, coiled segments. The yarn is formed in a similar way to a looped yarn, by holding two singles at differing gauges and allowing one to wrap tightly around the tense central core.

Knots, or knops, can be made in a similar way, with one single held tense and the remaining thread or threads delivered in greater quantities at certain intervals, making a coiled bunch, or knot of fiber.

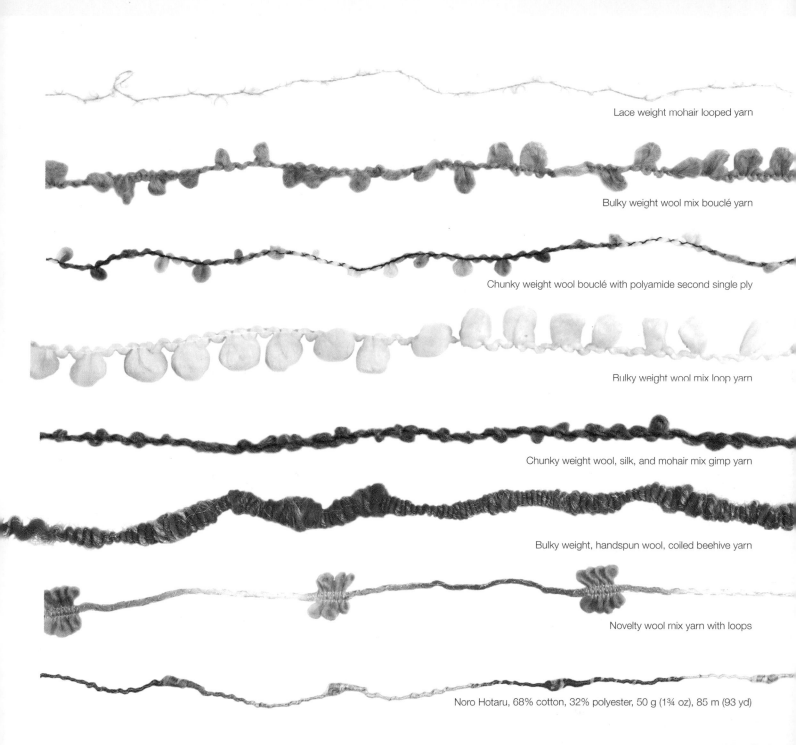

Lace weight mohair looped yarn

Bulky weight wool mix bouclé yarn

Chunky weight wool bouclé with polyamide second single ply

Bulky weight wool mix loop yarn

Chunky weight wool, silk, and mohair mix gimp yarn

Bulky weight, handspun wool, coiled beehive yarn

Novelty wool mix yarn with loops

Noro Hotaru, 68% cotton, 32% polyester, 50 g (1¾ oz), 85 m (93 yd)

Beaded yarns

Yarns can also have other materials added, which are not necessarily fibers at all. Beads, crystals, and sequins can be threaded onto a central core at intervals and spun within the fiber to create a single thread, out of which beads protrude. This type can also be made as a plied yarn, by plying the beaded thread together with one or more other singles.

Other ornamentation, such as small ribbons and other small snippets of fabric, can also be added to yarns when they are spun, by trapping them between two single plies. However, these can produce unstable yarns, with the added extras prone to falling off the final fabric.

A yarn made in a similar way to this is fur yarn, which is created by trapping many loose, long hairlike strands between the two binding single plies. Unsurprisingly, it knits up to resemble an animal's fur. Eyelash yarn tends to give a sparser version of fur, with long, hairlike strands. It is usually bound together with very fine plies, making it thin and flimsy to work with, often easier to knit alongside another yarn to add texture and to define the stitches. Be careful if using these unstable yarns for baby clothing or toys, because the threads can come off in a baby's mouth.

Tapes and ribbons

A ribbon yarn is a woven fabric strip, which is an extra-long and often more pliable version of what you usually expect a ribbon to be.

A tape is a single-ply narrow fabric as well, and knits to good effect. A tape can also describe a tube of knitting. Nonspun yarns such as these are a fantastic opportunity for experimentation. It is easy and fun to create your own yarns from ribbons and fabric and other remnants you may find lying around in your stash. Cut up fabric into strips and knit with it, or alternatively, there are ready-cut recycled fabric "yarns" on the market. Another idea is to use a sewing machine to sew together little scraps of fabric and yarn or ribbon to create your own chenille-like yarn.

Nonspun yarns

Chenille is a velvety yarn with a luxurious pile created from a woven fabric with many runs, cut to form loose ends. Chenille often sheds from these loose ends.

Yarns come in an endless variety of textures and colors.

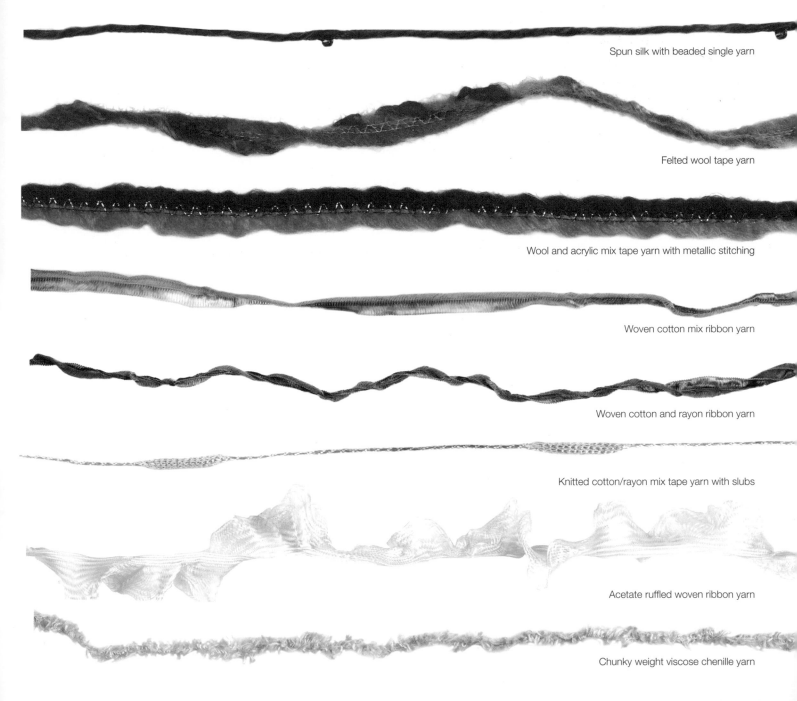

Spun silk with beaded single yarn

Felted wool tape yarn

Wool and acrylic mix tape yarn with metallic stitching

Woven cotton mix ribbon yarn

Woven cotton and rayon ribbon yarn

Knitted cotton/rayon mix tape yarn with slubs

Acetate ruffled woven ribbon yarn

Chunky weight viscose chenille yarn

Yarn weights

The thickness of yarn is called the weight. The classifications will vary from country to country and yarn to yarn but can be roughly arranged in groups.

Laceweight/2– or 3–ply

The gauge of these extra-fine yarns, often mohair for lace knitting, varies greatly.

Superfine/fingering weight/sock/4–ply

Often described as baby weight and used most commonly in children's clothing, Fair Isle, and sock knitting, this fine-weight yarn knits up to approximately 27–32 sts to 4 in (10 cm).

Fine/sportweight/baby

Also used in baby clothes, this in-between weight knits to 23–26 sts to 4 in (10 cm).

8–ply/double knitting/light

Double knitting, or DK, is a versatile, common thickness of yarn, with many uses. DK knits to roughly 21–24 sts per 4 in (10 cm).

Medium/fisherman/worsted weight/12–ply

A weight often used traditionally for cables and "Aran" knitting. Gauge is roughly 16–20 sts to 4 in (10 cm).

Bulky/chunky

A much thicker yarn, used mainly for winter clothing, with a gauge of about 12–15 sts to 4 in (10 cm).

Super bulky

The thickest of weights, knitted on very large needles, giving a gauge of 6–11 sts to 4 in (10 cm).

Needle sizes vary in the US and Europe, so check which system your pattern uses.

Tip

Vintage patterns may use Imperial English sizes, so beware!

Knitting needles

Modern needles are usually made of lightweight metal, wood, bamboo, or plastic and are supplied in a comprehensive range of sizes, both in diameter and length. In most cases, the size will be marked either on the side of the needle or on the "stopper" at the end. The size of the needles required for any project is determined by the thickness of the yarn and the number of stitches the project requires.

The choice of material is down mainly to personal preference. However, some materials will be particularly suited to certain yarns, fibers, or projects. For example, steel and aluminum needles are slippery and therefore good for fluffy or "sticky" yarns such as mohair, while bamboo needles are slightly "grippier" so are better for slippery yarns like silk. Double-pointed needles are sets of four or five needles, pointed at both ends.

Circular needles

Circular knitting needles are two short needles joined together by a cord. They (like double-pointed needles) allow you to knit "in the round" to produce tubular knitting such as socks. When working in the round, you need to work only knit or plain rows (see page 44) because your work is not turned at the end of each row. However, circular needles can also be used in the same way as a pair of traditional needles by working knit and purl rows and turning the work at the end of each row. They are especially useful in this case when you are working wide projects with lots of stitches, such as blankets.

Needle sizes

The US uses its own system for differentiating needle size (US size). Otherwise, knitting needle size is given in millimeters (mm) in Europe, and measures the diameter of the shaft of the needle; therefore, the larger the number, the thicker the needle. International knitting magazines and books should give needle sizes in both mm and in US size. You will need all the knitting needles stated in the pattern if you knit to the gauge the designer has given. Edges and hems are in general knitted on a smaller needle, and long edges may require a circular needle to fit all the stitches.

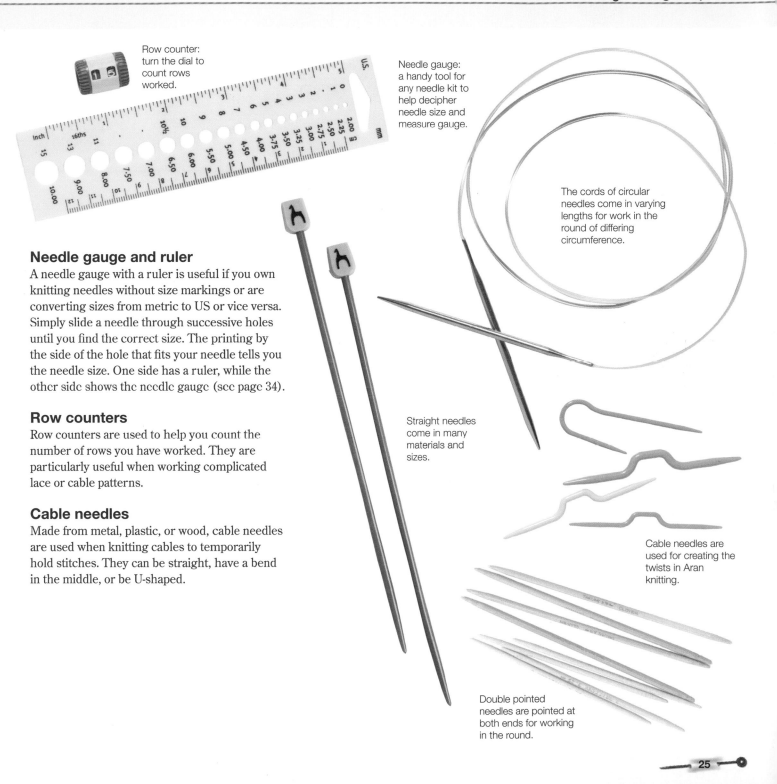

Row counter: turn the dial to count rows worked.

Needle gauge: a handy tool for any needle kit to help decipher needle size and measure gauge.

The cords of circular needles come in varying lengths for work in the round of differing circumference.

Needle gauge and ruler

A needle gauge with a ruler is useful if you own knitting needles without size markings or are converting sizes from metric to US or vice versa. Simply slide a needle through successive holes until you find the correct size. The printing by the side of the hole that fits your needle tells you the needle size. One side has a ruler, while the other side shows the needle gauge (see page 34).

Row counters

Row counters are used to help you count the number of rows you have worked. They are particularly useful when working complicated lace or cable patterns.

Cable needles

Made from metal, plastic, or wood, cable needles are used when knitting cables to temporarily hold stitches. They can be straight, have a bend in the middle, or be U-shaped.

Straight needles come in many materials and sizes.

Cable needles are used for creating the twists in Aran knitting.

Double pointed needles are pointed at both ends for working in the round.

Other equipment

People who knit regularly end up acquiring a range of tools and equipment designed to make the process easier and more accurate. The pages that follow take you through the basics you will encounter on knitting websites and in stores. There are many more items available and you will end up personalizing your own kit, but these are the essentials.

Scissors and tape measure

A pair of small, sharp scissors is an essential tool for trimming loose yarn ends (see page 27). As you make a knitted project, you will often be required to take measurements. It is a good idea to have a tape measure that has inches and centimeters clearly marked on the same side.

A tape measure is essential for monitoring length as you knit

Stitch holders

You will find these particularly useful where stitches need to be left unworked in order to work later on. Stitches can unravel easily when slipped off a knitting needle so a safety pin or stitch holder is helpful for keeping stitches from dropping (see page 27). The stitches slip from the knitting needle onto the holder in the same way as you would slip a stitch from one needle to another (see Slipping a knit stitch and Slipping a purl stitch, page 52).

Point protectors

These protect the points of your knitting needles and keep your knitting from slipping off the needles when you are not working on your project.

Pins and needles

Choose pins with brightly colored tips, as they are much easier to see. The most common pins found in stores are the plastic-headed straight pins most commonly used for dressmaking—these are fine if you need to pin only a small area. It is also possible to buy specific knitters' pins that are longer and thicker and have large, flat heads—these tend to be a little more stable than dressmaking pins.

Knitters' sewing or tapestry needles come in various sizes. The eye needs to be large enough to accommodate the knitting yarn, and the point should be relatively blunt.

Stitch markers

Stitch markers are used as an alternative to knitters' pins and are extremely useful for counting stitches and pattern repeats (see page 27) as well as marking the beginning of a round in circular knitting. They can be slipped through a knitted stitch and caught onto the yarn, or placed over the knitting needle when beginning a large cast-on or working in the round.

Yarn bobbins

When using different colors in a Fair Isle or intarsia design, you may find it easier to wind small amounts of yarn around a bobbin instead of working directly from the ball, to prevent tangling.

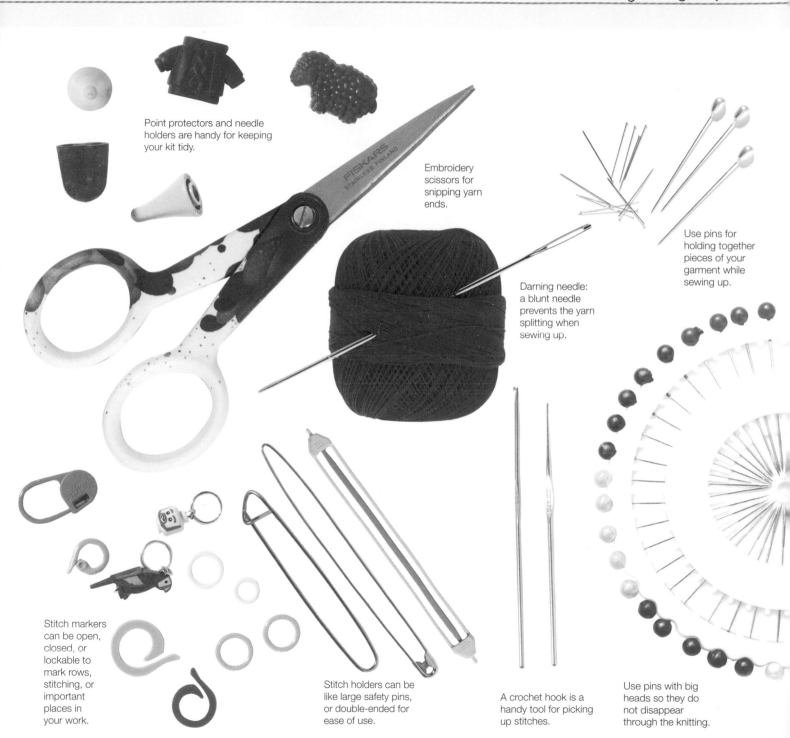

Point protectors and needle holders are handy for keeping your kit tidy.

Embroidery scissors for snipping yarn ends.

Use pins for holding together pieces of your garment while sewing up.

Darning needle: a blunt needle prevents the yarn splitting when sewing up.

Stitch markers can be open, closed, or lockable to mark rows, stitching, or important places in your work.

Stitch holders can be like large safety pins, or double-ended for ease of use.

A crochet hook is a handy tool for picking up stitches.

Use pins with big heads so they do not disappear through the knitting.

Substituting yarns

There are some fabulous yarns to choose from these days, so don't fall into the trap of thinking that you have to use the exact yarn or color specified in a pattern. When substituting yarn, it is, however, important that you stick to the same weight of yarn.

Substituting yarn can be one of the most confusing things when following a pattern. If you want to use a different yarn to the one stated in the pattern and don't want to adapt the pattern at all, you must look for a yarn in a similar weight (or thickness) to the one stated, otherwise the knitting will give a different gauge and the garment may come out the wrong size. The many types and weights of yarn can be confusing (see pages 22–23 as a guide), but it is easiest to look at the gauge the pattern calls for and check the ball band (see opposite) for a yarn that gives a similar gauge.

The next factor you must take into consideration is the drape of the yarn suggested. You will get a very different-looking fabric unless you use a similar fiber, for example heavy yarns such as cotton will hang very differently from lofty, fluffy, and light woolen yarns. The stitch definition and color choice are also important—there is

no reason to knit a complex stitch if the pattern does not show up well on the final garment. The most important tip is to always work a gauge swatch (or four!) before you begin with a new yarn.

If you do decide to use a substitute yarn, consider the yardage of each ball. For example, if the pattern requires ten balls of wool and each ball contains 130 yd (120 m) of yarn, then the total yardage of the project is 1,300 yd (1,200 m). If the substitute yarn has only 90 yd (82 m) per ball, you will need more than ten balls. To calculate how many more, divide the total yardage (1,300) by the substitute ball yardage (90):

$$1300 \div 90 = 15.$$

If in doubt, always buy a little extra.

Ball-band information

Most yarns have a ball band or tag of some sort that gives you all the information you will need about the yarn. The heading on the band shows the company logo, the specific name of the yarn, and often the yarn weight.

The band will also tell you what fiber the yarn is made from—cotton, wool, etc. The weight and the approximate length of the yarn will also be shown. Most yarns sold commercially come in certain weights, usually 1¾ oz (50 g) or 3½ oz (100 g), although it is possible to purchase yarn in larger amounts, especially when using acrylic yarns, which are sometimes sold in 7-oz (200-g) balls.

There may be symbols or written instructions on washing and drying guidelines, and the shade and dye-lot number on the ball band.

It is important that all of the yarn for a project comes from the same dye lot. Slight differences in color may not be immediately apparent, but could be horribly obvious in a knitted piece.

The most important piece of information is the graph that shows the knitting gauge and the guide to needle sizes. In this case, you should knit to a gauge of 19–20 stitches and 28 rows to 4 in/10 cm on size 6–7 (4–4.5 mm) needles (see pages 34–35).

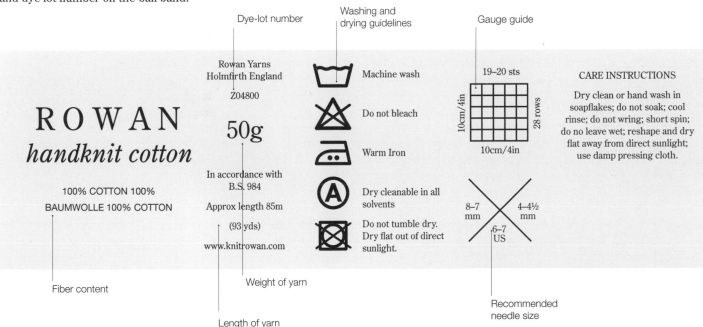

Dye-lot number

Washing and drying guidelines

Gauge guide

Rowan Yarns
Holmfirth England

Z04800

ROWAN
handknit cotton

100% COTTON 100%
BAUMWOLLE 100% COTTON

50g

In accordance with
B.S. 984

Approx length 85m

(93 yds)

www.knitrowan.com

Machine wash

Do not bleach

Warm Iron

Dry cleanable in all solvents

Do not tumble dry. Dry flat out of direct sunlight.

19–20 sts

10cm/4in

28 rows

10cm/4in

CARE INSTRUCTIONS

Dry clean or hand wash in soapflakes; do not soak; cool rinse; do not wring; short spin; do no leave wet; reshape and dry flat away from direct sunlight; use damp pressing cloth.

8–7 mm

4–4½ mm

6–7 US

Fiber content

Weight of yarn

Length of yarn

Recommended needle size

Washing and care essentials

When knitted in a quality yarn and cared for in the correct manner, hand-knit garments can last for many years. Keep the ball band so you can refer to it when you need to launder the knitted fabric. Before making any decisions about how to care for an item, always check the ball band for as much information as possible.

Can be machine washed

Hand wash only

Do not iron

Before immersing the item in water, remove any nonwashable trims, such as buttons or braid. Avoid using washing powders with any kind of added brighteners. Soap flakes, mild detergent, and specially formulated liquids are usually best.

Make sure the water is cool and the detergent is completely dissolved. If the detergent needs warm or hot water in order to disperse thoroughly, make sure it has had time to cool before you begin. Wash one garment at a time and change the water after every piece. Do not wring, twist, or rub the fabric, and never use a brush to remove spots or stains. Wash the garment as quickly as possible, although some pieces can be left to soak for short lengths of time. Make sure the water runs clear after the final rinse.

To remove most of the water from your garment, lay it out flat on a towel, roll up the towel, and press firmly on the resulting sausage shape until all the excess is squeezed gently into the towel. If you are machine-washing a knitted project, use a delicate or wool cold-water cycle with minimal fast spin action. It is preferable to put delicate garments in a net bag or tied pillowcase before spinning.

Drying

Never hang your hand-knit garment to dry as it will stretch, sometimes to ridiculous lengths. When drying, block the garment by laying it out on a clean, dry towel and pin lightly to size if it needs to be reshaped. Let it dry away from direct sunlight or heat sources. Careful blocking of a damp knitted piece should eliminate the need to steam or press it once dry, which is desirable, as pressing knitted stitches can flatten them.

Always dry your hand-knitted garments flat.

Blocking

In a similar way to drying your finished garments, it is amazing how much can be achieved to neaten your finished knitted pieces with simple blocking techniques.

Blocking must always be done prior to sewing up the pieces, to ensure all are the same size and do not become misshapen once sewn together. Basic garment pieces can sometimes be simply pinned to shape and then lightly steamed with an iron set to "steam shot" to set the stitches, but a word of warning: do not press with the iron, as this will flatten the fabric; simply hover it over the surface and allow the steam to work its magic.

With lace, and with any piece that has for some reason been knitted to the wrong measurements, you must block the pieces carefully. You can buy specialist blocking wires, which are especially good for large lace pieces such as shawls or scarves, but you can also achieve the same effect by pinning to a towel or your ironing board.

Large-headed pins are the best type to use when blocking and working with yarn in general, because the colored heads won't get lost between the stitches.

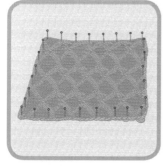

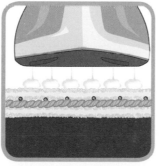

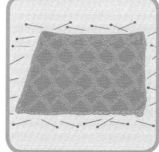

1 To do this, you must lay each piece, with the right side facing down, onto a clean, very slightly damp towel and pin to shape as with drying (see page 30). If you wish to ensure two identical pieces are the exact same size and shape, pin them on top of each other as a guide.

2 Lay another damp towel over the top and lightly pass over an iron, without pressing, but with the "full steam" option selected. You must let the steam and moisture do the work, rather than the weight of the iron, as this will flatten the stitches and create an ugly final fabric.

3 Once the whole piece is warmed and steamed thoroughly, let it cool down and dry completely, then you can unpin and remove the pieces.

Tip

You must never iron complex cables or ribbing, even lightly, as this will destroy their innate properties. You can simply leave the blocked, damp pieces to dry completely without steaming.

How to read a pattern

There is certain information contained in every written pattern, regardless of the company that has produced it, and it is important that you read through the entire pattern before starting to knit any project to ensure that you understand all of the abbreviations.

Patterns are often written for more than one size and will express these as age, dress size, or chest/bust measurement. In this book, the smallest size is shown first, with subsequent sizes shown in parentheses. The same principle applies for yarn quantities, numbers of stitches, and any other measurements. There should also be at least three finished measurements given. These are the chest/bust measurement taken under the arms, the length from the shoulder to the bottom edge, and the sleeve length from the beginning of the cuff to the widest point of the sleeve top. In some cases there may be a schematic drawing showing these measurements and the general shape of the garment. To avoid any mistakes when following a pattern with more than one size, it is a good idea to circle all figures for the size you wish to make before you commence. Yarn amounts, needle sizes, and any extra equipment and materials will also appear at the beginning of a pattern.

Selecting size

It is best to go by the actual size measurements given in the pattern, rather than the "to fit bust…/chest…/size 8." Some patterns give an actual size, while others just print it using a small schematic drawing. The reason for this is that there is ease to take into account. This is the difference between your size and the actual size of the garment. Usually, the ease is positive. Some garments will be close fitting (choose a size from the actual size of your bust/chest to about 1½ in/4 cm larger), standard fitting (2–4 in/5–10 cm bigger), loose fitting (4–6 in/10–15 cm bigger), and oversize (anything over 6 in/15 cm bigger). There is also negative ease, which is where a garment is less than the size of your body; as knitting stretches, the garment will expand to fit the contours of the figure.

Abbreviations

The patterns in this book feature a number of standard abbreviations, which are explained below.
These abbreviations are logical and easy to understand.

alt	alternate	**kwise**	knitwise	**rem**	remain/remaining	**St st**	stockinette stitch/stocking stitch
beg	begin(s)/beginning	**LH**	left hand	**rep**	repeat(s)		
BO	bind off	**LHN**	left hand needle	**rev St st**	reverse stockinette stitch	**tbl**	through back loop
CC	contrasting color	**lp(s)**	loop(s)			**tog**	together
cm	centimeter(s)	**M1**	make 1 stitch	**RH**	right hand	**WS**	wrong side
cn	cable needle	**M1 p-st**	make 1 stitch purlwise	**RS**	right side	**WSR**	wrong side row
cont	continue			**RHN**	right hand needle	**wyib**	with yarn in back
CO	cast on	**MC**	main color	**rnd(s)**	round(s)	**wyif**	with yarn in front
dec	decrease(s)/decreasing	**mm**	millimeters	**RSF**	right side facing	**yfwd**	yarn forward
		p	purl	**RSR**	right side row	**yo**	yarn over
DPN(s)	double pointed needle(s)	**patt**	pattern(s)	**sk**	skip	**yon**	yarn over needle
foll	follow(s)/following	**psso**	pass slipped stitch over	**sl**	slip	**yrn**	yarn around needle
in	inch(es)	**p2sso**	pass two slipped sts over	**sl1k**	slip one knitwise		
inc	increase(s)/increasing	**p2tog**	purl two stitches together	**sl1p**	slip one purlwise		
incl	inclusive	**pm**	place marker	**sl st**	slip stitch		
k	knit	**prev**	previous	**ssk**	slip, slip, knit these two stitches together—a decrease		
k1b	knit one below	**pwise**	purlwise				
k2tog	knit two stitches			**st(s)**	stitch(es)		

Tip

When choosing which size garment to knit, measure an existing garment that fits you really well and compare it to the measurements given in the pattern. By choosing the size that has the closest measurements to an existing garment, you can be sure of getting the right fit.

Correct gauge
The gauge is correct, therefore the sample piece is the correct size.

Gauge swatches

It is very important that your knitted project is worked to the correct gauge. This means that the number of stitches measured over a specified distance (usually 4 in/10 cm) matches those instructed on the ball band or by the pattern.

It is very important to knit a gauge swatch before beginning a project to ensure that it turns out the correct size and shape. The pattern will list the number of stitches and rows to 4 in (10 cm). If you find you have more stitches and rows to 4 in (10 cm), use a larger knitting needle. If you have worked fewer stitches and rows, use a smaller needle to achieve the correct gauge.

The diameter of the knitting needle affects the size of the stitch, so stitches knitted on a chunky needle will take up more space than those knitted on a fine one. Be aware that your own personal gauge is linked to technique and can change with practice. It can even be dependent on your mood or the situation in which you are knitting!

If you have knitted too tightly or too loosely, then your finished project will be the wrong size. Not only that, but the amount of yarn that you require to complete the project will change. It is important to work a gauge swatch before you embark on any knitted project.

Too loose
The gauge is too loose, therefore the sample piece is too large.

Too tight
The gauge is too tight, therefore the sample piece is too small.

Measuring and counting gauge

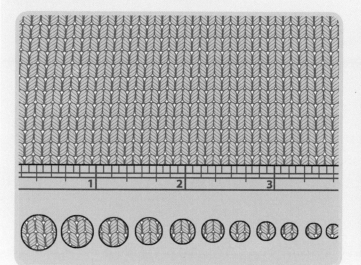

1 Lay your knitted gauge swatch flat. Using a flat ruler (or tape measure), measure across a horizontal row of stitches and place a marker pin at the 4 in/10 cm point. Do the same for the vertical rows of stitches.

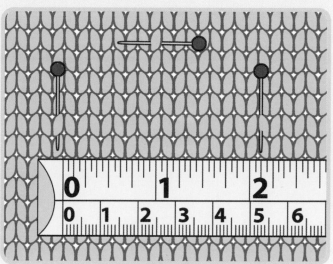

2 Use the point of a knitting needle or pencil to count the number of stitches and rows between each pin.

How to knit a gauge swatch

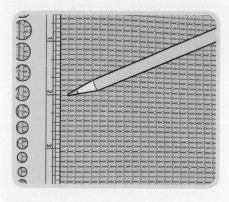

A gauge swatch is used to ensure you are knitting at the gauge called for in the pattern. This is essential in order to achieve the right size of garment. To do this, you need to knit a small square of just over 4 x 4 in (10 x 10 cm) in the main yarn and stitch used in the pattern, then count the average number of stitches and rows per in/cm. Cast on more stitches and work more rows than the gauge in the pattern suggests. This way a true gauge is achieved within the square, as the edge stitches can often be distorted. When you have completed the swatch, take a measuring tape or ruler and take some average measurements—count how many stitches and rows to 4 in/10 cm, at different points over the swatch. To make this easier, place pins at the 0–in/cm line and the 4–in/10–cm line, then count the amount of stitches/rows between the pins.

Holding the needles

A knitted fabric is created by working combinations of just two different stitches on a pair of knitting needles after a cast-on row. The way the needles are held can vary, but the most common positions are shown below.

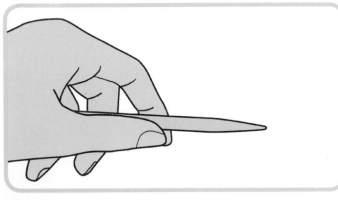

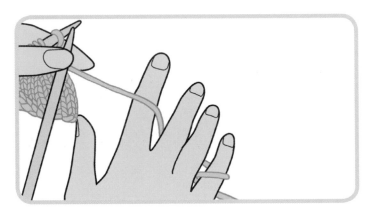

English method
The left hand takes the weight of the needles while the stitch is being made. The yarn is held in the right hand and wraps around the right needle.

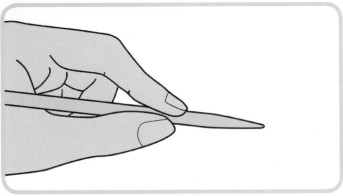

How to hold the needles
There is no absolute correct way to hold your needles, and everyone has his or her own variation, but there are two more common ways of holding the needles: like a pen or like a knife. You may find that both hands want to hold the needles in the same way, but if it is comfortable, you can hold each needle in a different way.

Continental method
The yarn is held in the left hand and the right needle "picks" the yarn from the left hand.

Making a slip knot

A knitted fabric is made by working rows of stitches in various sequences. In order to create a fabric, you must first make a base row, known as a cast-on row. A slip knot is used as the first stitch for a cast-on row.

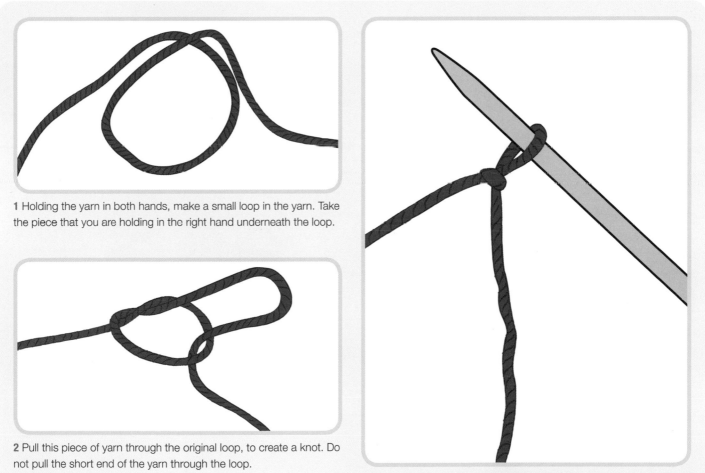

1 Holding the yarn in both hands, make a small loop in the yarn. Take the piece that you are holding in the right hand underneath the loop.

2 Pull this piece of yarn through the original loop, to create a knot. Do not pull the short end of the yarn through the loop.

3 Place the slip knot onto the knitting needle.

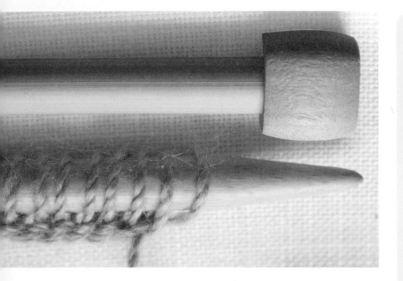

Casting on

Casting on is the first step in hand knitting and it provides the first row of loops on the needle. Different methods of casting on produce different types of edges, each with its own appropriate use, and it is advisable to practice all of these variations at some stage.

When a pattern does not state which cast on edge to use, simply use your favorite cast on, although some cast ons will be more appropriate to certain projects than others.

The thumb method

This method is perfect for creating a stretchy edge for an edge where elasticity is required, such as a ribbed cuff. You cannot use it in the middle of the work — try the two-needle or cable method. If you are a continental knitter, you will not be able to work this cast on; try the continental method instead for an alternative.

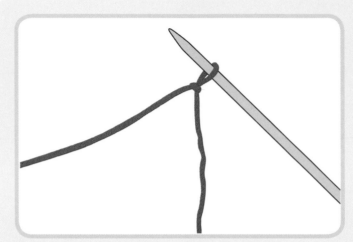

1 Make a slip knot into your yarn, leaving a long tail of approximately three times the length of the desired width of your fabric. Place the slip knot onto the needle and hold needle in your right hand.

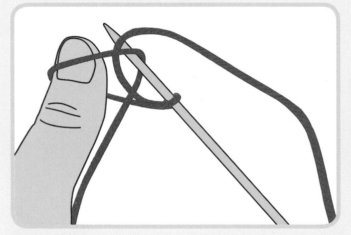

4 Wrap ball end of yarn around right-hand needle as if knitting normally.

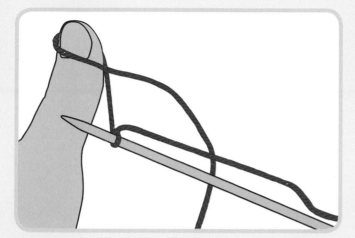

2 Grab the long tail loose end of the yarn in your left hand and make a loop around your left thumb with this end, still holding tight to the loose end.

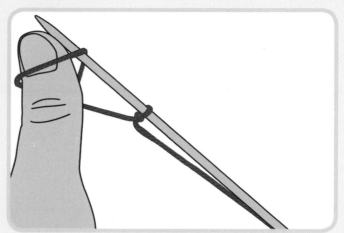

3 With the left thumb upright, slip right-hand needle through the loop made around the thumb from bottom to top.

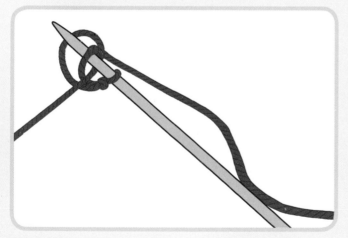

5 Draw the loop just made around the needle through the loop on the thumb.

6 This is the resulting cast on stitch alongside the slip knot. Now repeat steps 2–5 for desired amount of stitches.

The cable method

This cast-on method uses both knitting needles and creates a strong edge with a double thickness of yarn. You do not need to allow for a tail end of yarn, as in the thumb method. The ball end of the yarn is held in the right hand, but the tail end of the yarn is not used and therefore can be short.

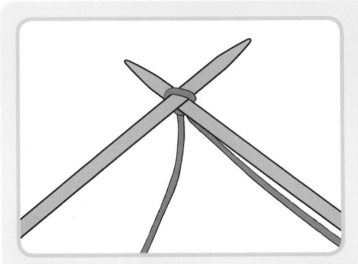

1 Place the slip knot onto the knitting needle and hold the needle in your left hand. Slide the right knitting needle through the loop created by the slip knot from front to back.

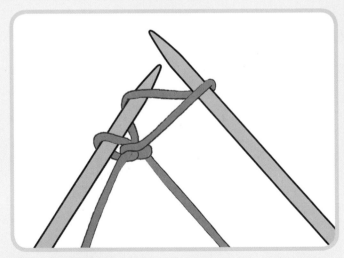

4 Pass the left needle over the top of the new loop, placing the tip of the needle through the loop on the right needle. Remove the right needle, thus transferring the stitch to the left needle.

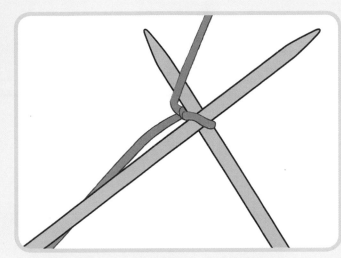

2 With your right hand, wrap the yarn around the right knitting needle counterclockwise from back to front.

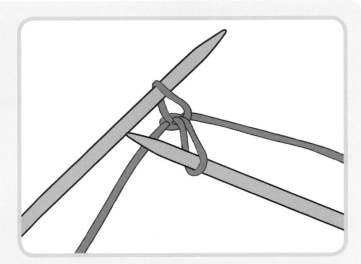

3 Slide the right needle through the loop on the left needle, catching the wrapped yarn and bringing it through the loop to create another loop.

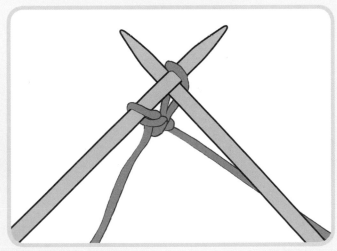

5 Make each subsequent stitch by placing the right needle between the last two stitches made on the left needle, and repeating steps 2 through 4.

The continental cast on

The continental method is an alternative way to create the elastic thumb method and can be worked by English or continental knitters. It is also called the long-tail or double cast-on method.

As with the thumb method, you need to leave a tail of approx 3–5 times as long as the desired cast on edge. The method uses one needle held in the right hand and your left hand holding the two strands of yarn — the short tail and the ball end.

Continental cast on
The continental method is perfect for continental knitters.

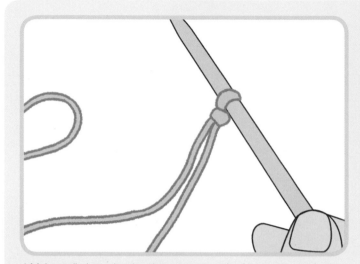

1 Make a slip knot, leaving the correct length of long tail and place on right needle.

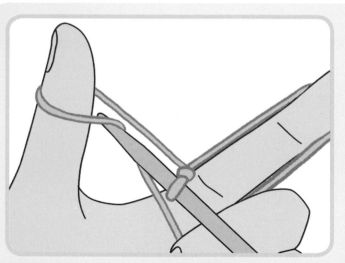

4 Bring needle up through loop on thumb from bottom.

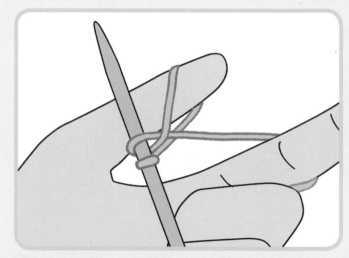

5 Draw loop from thumb up and grab a strand from around index finger with needle.

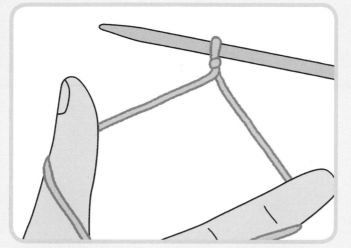

2 Grab both ends of yarn in your hand, with long tail on left, ball end to the right. Place thumb and index finger of left hand between yarn ends so that working yarn is around index finger and tail end is around thumb, making a diamond shape with the yarn.

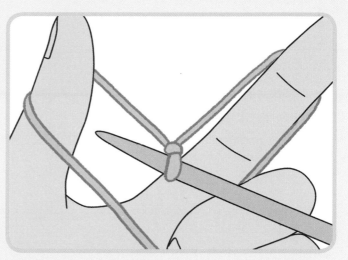

3 Pull needle downward to create a "heart" type shape with the yarn.

6 Draw loop from index finger back down through loop on thumb to create a stitch on the needle.

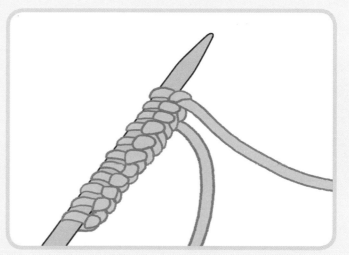

7 Drop loop off thumb and, placing thumb back through the center of the two strands of yarn in the diamond configuration, tighten resulting stitch on needle. Rep steps 2– 7 until you have cast on desired number of stitches.

Knit and purl stitches

Most knitting is based on combinations of just two basic stitches—knit stitch and purl stitch. Once you have mastered these two stitches, you can work many different stitch patterns.

Begin by casting on about 25–30 stitches using one of the methods on pages 38–43.

Knit stitch

Practice knit stitch until you can work it fairly smoothly, then practice purl stitch. The knit stitch is the simplest of all stitches. Knitting every row forms the ridged fabric called garter stitch. With knitting, the aim is to hold the needle with the stitches in your left hand, and transfer them all to the right needle by knitting another row.

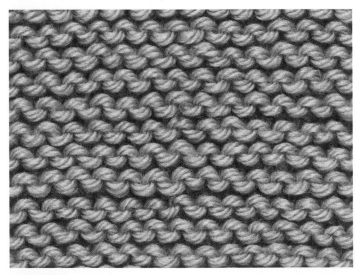

Garter stitch.

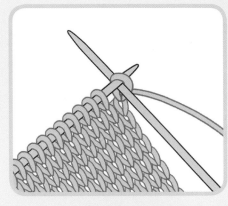

1 Hold the needle with the stitches to be knitted in the left hand with the yarn behind the work.

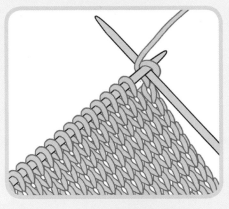

2 Insert the right-hand needle into a stitch from front to back. Take the yarn over it, forming a loop.

3 Bring the needle and the new loop to the front of the work through the stitch, and slide the original stitch off the left-hand needle.

Purl stitch

This is the second basic knitting stitch you learn. When you use purl in a fabric, you never work every row purl, as this fabric would look exactly the same as garter stitch, and as the purl stitch is slightly more difficult, this is pointless. You usually work a row of purls followed by a row of knits, then alternate knit and purl every row, which is called stockinette stitch.

Stockinette stitch.

The reverse side of stockinette stitch.

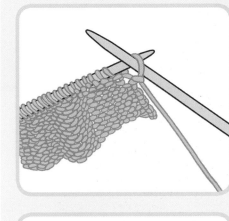

1 Hold the stitches to be purled in the left hand, with the yarn at the front of the work.

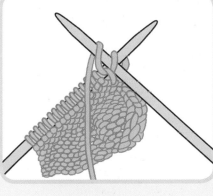

2 Insert the right-hand needle through the front of the stitch, from right to left. Take the yarn over and under, forming a loop.

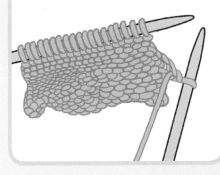

3 Take the needle and the new loop through the back and slide the stitch off the left-hand needle.

Binding off

There is one simple and commonly used method of securing stitches once you have finished a piece of knitting: binding off. There are various methods of achieving this, a couple of examples of which are shown here. These captions show casting off along a knit row. However, you can cast off in pattern along any fabric, simply working each stitch as set in pattern, instead of knitting all stitches across the row.

Cable bind-off

Cable bind-off is a neat and tidy way of securing all the stitches so that they do not slip out of the last row worked. You achieve a cable bind-off using the two needles you have been knitting with all along.

Tip

It is important to remember that the bound-off edge should have the same amount of elasticity as the rest of the fabric.

If your bound-off edge is too tight, use a larger needle.

Always bind off in the same stitch as the pattern, unless advised otherwise.

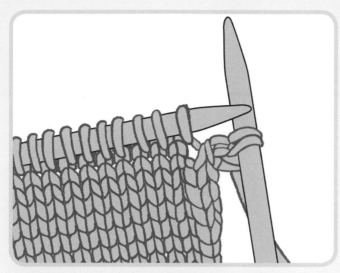

1 At the point where you are ready to bind off, knit the first two stitches.

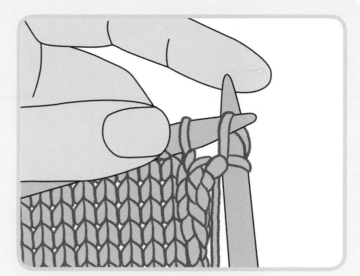

2 Slip the left-hand needle into the first stitch on the right-hand needle, and lift it over the second stitch and off the needle.

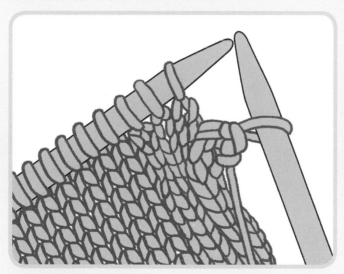

3 Knit next stitch so that there are two stitches on the right-hand needle again.

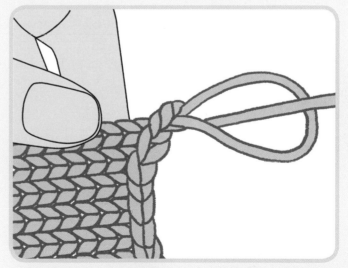

4 Repeat steps 2 and 3 until all stitches are knitted from left-hand needle and one stitch remains on right-hand needle. Make last stitch loop larger, break yarn and draw firmly through last stitch to fasten off.

Binding off seams together

To avoid having to use a sewing needle to join two bound-off edges, the two pieces—provided there are the same amount of stitches on each section—can be bound off together. This gives a very neat edge, and can save a lot of time. Leave stitches on a spare needle at the end instead of binding them off. Use the following method to join the pieces together.

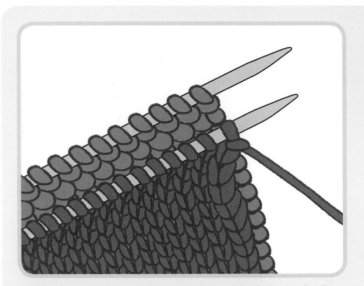

1 Place the knit pieces together with wrong sides facing each other.

4 Repeat steps 2 and 3 to create another stitch on the right-hand needle.

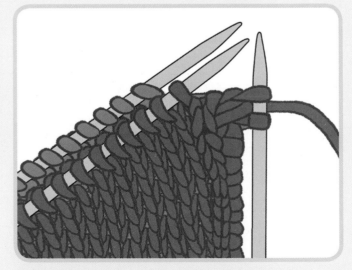

5 Work until you have two stitches on the right-hand needle.

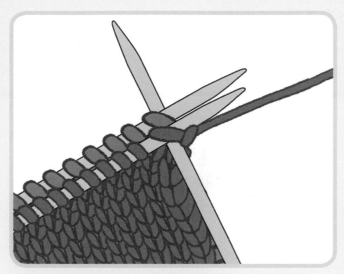

2 Using the same size needle as was used in the main part of the knitting, knit together the first stitch from the front needle with the first stitch from the back needle.

3 Draw the stitch through the two loops as you normally would when knitting, and drop the two stitches off the left-hand needle, leaving one stitch on the right-hand needle.

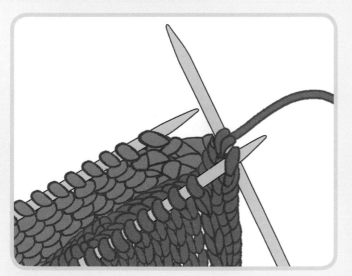

6 Bind off the right-hand stitch of the two, as you would when binding off single stitches.

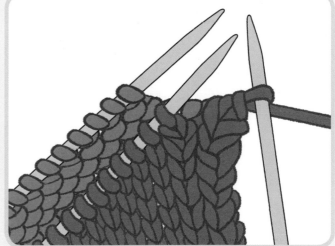

7 This will leave you with one stitch on your right-hand needle. Repeat from step 4 until all stitches are bound off.

Basic stitch variations

All knitting, however complicated, is made up of combinations of just two stitches: knit and purl. Clever combining of these two stitches, however, is the key to a world of variation in your knitting.

Garter stitch

If you were to work rows of just knit, or rows of just purl stitches in succession, you would create a knitted fabric known as garter stitch. This is quite textural and sturdy and looks the same on both sides of the fabric.

Stockinette stitch

Stockinette stitch fabric is different on both sides and therefore has a right side, or front, and a wrong side, or back. The sides of the fabric are also respectively referred to as a knit side and a purl side.

The right side is smooth, and you will be able to see that the stitches create a zigzag effect. The wrong side is bumpy and looks a little like garter stitch.

To make a fabric using stockinette stitch, work rows of knit stitches and rows of purl stitches alternately. If you have the smooth side of the fabric facing you as you begin the row, you will need to work a knit row in order to keep the pattern correct. If you have the more textural side facing you at the beginning of the row, you will need to work a purl row.

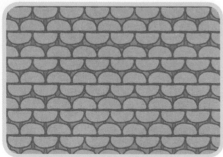

Garter stitch looks the same both sides

Stockinette stitch front or right side

Reverse stockinette stitch back or wrong side

Ribbing

A knit rib is simply a mix of knits and purls across a row. A rib can be any mix of knits and purls built up on top of each other in vertical lines or "ribs." A ribbed fabric is very stretchy and is therefore great in areas such as cuffs, where the fabric needs to grip more tightly to the body.

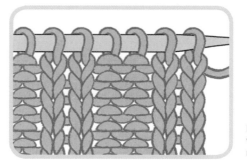

Ribbing is great when stretch is needed as for socks

Working knit and purl stitches in the same row

If you want to create textural relief patterns, you will need to work both knit and purl stitches in the same row. It is important that you change from a knit to a purl stitch and vice versa in the correct way.

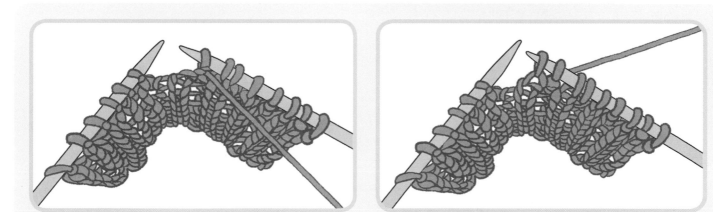

Changing from a purl stitch to a knit stitch Having completed a purl stitch, the yarn will be held at the front of the work. In order to work a subsequent knit stitch, take the yarn to the back of the work between both knitting needles. Then knit the next stitch.

Changing from a knit stitch to a purl stitch Having completed a knit stitch, the yarn will be held at the reverse of the work. In order to work a subsequent purl stitch, bring the yarn through to the front of the work between both knitting needles, then purl the next stitch.

Shaping knitting

To shape a knitted piece, you have to increase and decrease stitches. There are different ways of doing this and most knitters have their own preferences. Decreasing and increasing are also used to create a variety of stitches such as bobbles and lace patterns.

Patterns will often use different methods of increasing and decreasing for different parts of a pattern, due to the way in which differing stitches lie within the increase/decrease. For example, when shaping a raglan sleeve, it is preferable that the stitches lie in the direction of the shaping. Stitches on the right side of the raglan shaping need to form a slope that points to the left and stitches on the left side need to create a slope that points to the right. When these shapings are used as a feature, this is known as "fully fashioning."

Decreasing

You may be required to decrease stitches by working two or more stitches together in techniques such as lacework and when shaping a knitted piece.

There are many differing ways to do this and the most common and simplest way is to knit or purl two or more stitches together as in the following instructions.

Slipping a stitch

In order to create some textural fabrics such as lace, or when shaping a piece of knitting, you may be required to slip stitches from one needle to another, without knitting them.

To slip a stitch knit wise:
1 Slide the right-hand needle through the next stitch on the left needle from front to back, as if to knit. Let the stitch drop from the left needle and pass it onto the right knitting needle without knitting.

To slip a stitch purl wise:
1 Slide the right-hand needle through the next stitch on the left needle from right to left as if to purl. Let the stitch drop from the left needle and pass it onto the right needle without knitting.

k2tog: Decreasing is most commonly done by working two or more stitches together to form one stitch. On a knit or right-side row this creates a slope to the right.

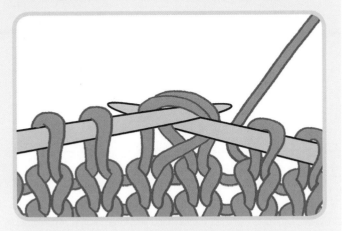

1 Slide the right needle through the second and then the first stitches on the left needle from front to back. Wrap the yarn around the right needle as a normal knit stitch.

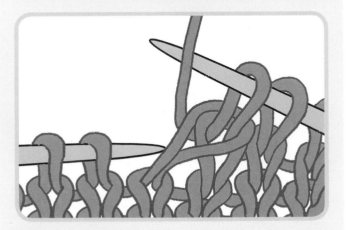

2 Knit the two stitches together as if knitting normally and slide both from the left needle.

p2tog: Working two or more stitches together on the wrong side of the knitted piece creates a slope to the right on the right side.

1 Slide the right needle through the first two stitches on the left needle "purlwise".

2 Purl the two stitches together as if purling normally and slide both from the left needle.

Shaping: Decreasing

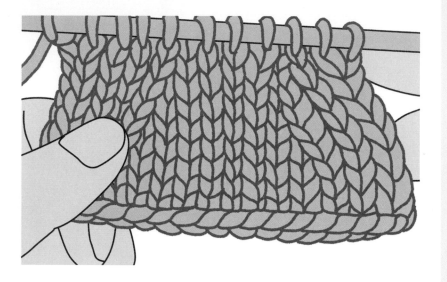

The ways of decreasing we have already practiced on previous pages create slopes to the right on the right side of the work. These mean that if you want to make a feature of these stitches, you would place them toward the left edge of your work to follow the right-leaning shaping.

Other ways of decreasing create slopes to the left on the right side of the work, so if you wanted to make a feature of these decreases in your work, you would position these decreases toward the right edge of your fabric, to follow the left-leaning shaping.

There are two different ways of creating a left-leaning decrease— either by working through the back of the loops or slipping and transferring stitches.

K2tog tbl

This is simply knitting two stitches together through the back loops of the stitches to twist them and cause a lean to the opposite side from k2tog.

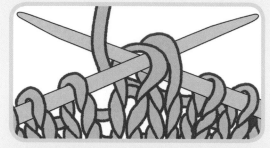

Work as for K2tog, but insert the right needle through the back loops of both stitches on the left needle; complete as for the regular k2tog.

p2tog tbl

This is simply purling two stitches together through the back loops of the stitches to twist them and cause a lean to the opposite direction to p2tog. This can be very fiddly to get right at first but practice makes perfect.

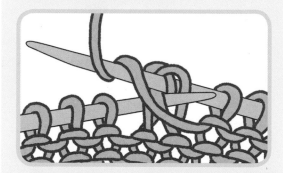

Insert the RHN through the back of the second, and then through the back of the first stitches on the LHN from left to right. Purl the two stitches together as for a regular p2tog and slide from the left needle.

ssk

This is simply slipping the next two stitches, then knitting them together—it is very similar to working a k2tog tbl but some find it easier to achieve.

S1, k1, psso/skpo

The slip one, knit one, pass slipped stitch over technique is probably the easiest of left-leaning decreasing techniques and is also abbreviated as skpo for brevity.

1 Slip the first stitch by placing the right needle through it as if knitting, and slide from the left needle. Knit the next stitch.

2 Using the left needle, pass the slipped stitch on the right needle over the top of the knitted stitch.

Slip next two sts knitwise onto right-hand needle.

Insert LHN into front of both sts from left to right.

Knit both sts tog.

Increasing

There are many ways to increase, and most knitters have their own favorite method. Increasing is usually done on the right side of the work. Patterns do not always specify how to increase and may just give the instruction to "make" or increase a number of stitches: m1 or inc.

inc: This usually means knitting into the front and then the back of a stitch. This increase is best worked at either the beginning or end of the knitted piece, as it is not very neat.

1 Work to where the extra stitch is needed. Knit into the front of the next stitch on the left knitting needle without slipping it off.

2 With the stitch still on the left needle and the yarn at the back, knit into the back of the same stitch and slip it from the needle.

m1: This is usually done by knitting into the back of the bar between stitches. It is a neat increase worked between two stitches.

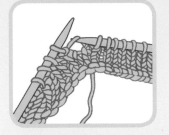

1 Pass the right knitting needle underneath the "bar" of yarn between two stitches from front to back.

2 Slip the loop onto the left needle and remove the right needle.

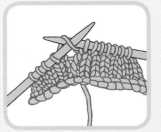

3 Knit into the back of the loop to twist it, by inserting the right needle behind the yarn on the left needle from right to left.

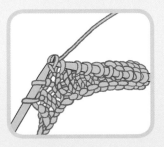

4 Finish the stitch as a normal knit stitch, remove the left needle, passing the new stitch onto the right needle.

Eyelet: This is the simplest way to make stitches. It creates a small hole, or eyelet, and is especially useful if you require a decorative detail.

1 Work to where the extra stitch is needed. Bring the yarn forward between both needles, take it over the right needle, and hold at the back. Knit the next stitch. Work in pattern to the end of the row.

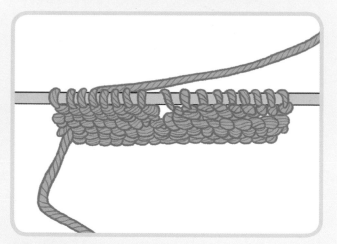

2 On the next row, knit or purl into the loop as if it were a normal stitch and continue in pattern to the end of the row.

Reverse shapings

When a pattern tells you to reverse shapings, it means you need to do the exact opposite of the side you have just knitted to the remaining part you have left to knit. For example, if you have been shaping the left side of a neckline (left side always refers to left side as if you were wearing the garment, not looking at it) you will have been using the k2tog decrease to get a shaping that leans to the right as you look at the neck; therefore, when you reattach the yarn to the right side of the neck, you need to decrease the same amount of stitches on the same rows as the right side, but on the neck edge, using a sl1, k1, psso, or ssk to create a slope to the left as you look at it.

Short row shaping/increasing by casting on

This is a form of shaping that creates flowing, neat curves and 3–D shapes within your flat knitting and can be achieved very easily. At its most basic, short rows are part-finished rows, creating stitches in parts of your knitting that are worked more frequently or for more rows than other stitches, meaning you're adding shaped rows into your work without adding or casting on extra stitches—you always have the same amount of stitches on the needle.

Short rows can be worked at the shoulder, to create a more elegant finish without such obvious 'steps'. They are perfect for a sock's heel, darts, and for making shawl collars.

A short row is created by working across to the allocated turn mark (or knitting the correct amount of stitches), then turning the work and leaving remaining stitches in the row unworked.

When you work a short row into the knit piece, you must make a smooth transition between the sides of the work with varying amounts of rows. Do this by wrapping a slipped stitch as follows.

Work to turn point, slip next stitch pwise onto right needle. Bring yarn to front.

Slip same stitch back to left needle unworked. Turn work and bring yarn into correct position for next stitch, wrapping the stitch as you do so.

Sometimes you can see these wrapped stitches, so if you wish you can hide them as follows.

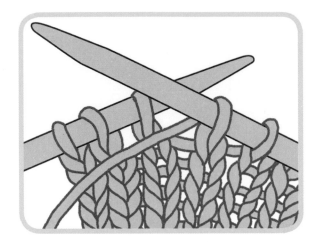

Knit stitch.

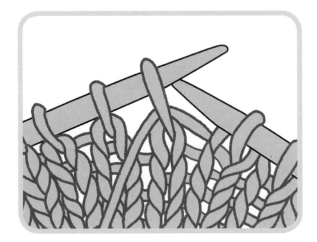

Purl stitch.

Knit stitch: On right side, work to just before wrapped stitch. Insert right needle from front, under the wrap from bottom up, and then into wrapped stitch as usual. Knit them together, making sure new stitch comes out under wrap.

Purl stitch: On wrong side, work to just before wrapped stitch. Insert right needle from back, under wrap from bottom up, and put on left needle. Purl them together.

Increasing by casting on

At the end of a row, if you need to increase a lot of stitches, you can simply cast them on by using the two-needle method outlined on pages 40–41.

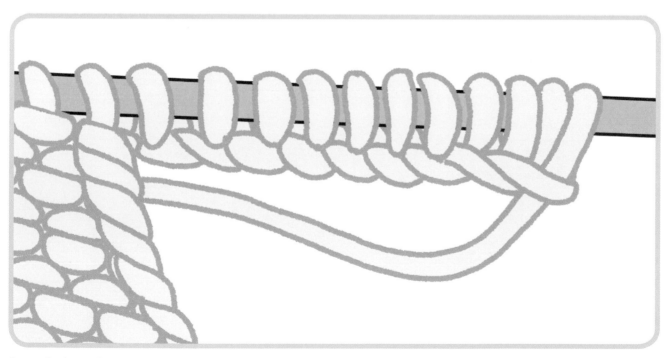

lincreasing by casting on.

Joining in a new yarn

When you have run out of yarn, you must tie in a new ball in the same way that you tie in a new color if you are striping. If you are knitting stripes, you must tie in the yarn at the start of a row, but when you are tying in the same color you can start anywhere across a row, although ends are easier to tie in and weave in at the edge of the work as opposed to in the center of it.

Joining a new yarn

1 Slide the right needle into the first stitch on the left needle, from front to back. Lay the new yarn over both needles with the tail end of the yarn to the back of the work.

2 Cross the finished end over the top of the new yarn and drop it.

3 Pick up the new end of yarn, holding the finished end securely in your right hand.

4 Using the new end of yarn, knit the stitch by taking it around the right needle counterclockwise.

5 Slide the right needle through the stitch on the left needle and under the tail end of yarn. Remove the left needle and allow the stitch to transfer to the right needle.

 Tip

This technique is the same, whether you are working a knit or a purl stitch; simply work whichever stitch is applicable.

Fixing mistakes

There are many mistakes to be made while knitting and it is interesting how beginners frequently make the same ones. When knitting straight, beginners often end up with slanting edges, caused by either adding or losing stitches.

While it is often assumed that it is more common to lose stitches, it is actually easier to gain them. To avoid this, try to count your stitches every row as you practice, to see if you can spot where the mistake has been made. Watch that you do not pass the yarn from front to back when it is not called for, knit into only the stitch on the needle, not into the stitch below, do not wrap the yarn twice around the needle when knitting, and always try to remember to drop off the final loop at the end of a stitch. When ribbing, remember to always move between the front and back of the work when you are working a mixture of knits and purls.

The best thing to do when learning is to take it very slowly and try not to get too distracted. By ensuring that you accurately count how many stitches there are at the beginning of a row, you will hopefully avoid the common mistake of counting the first stitch as two. This is easy to do when you are a beginner and the edge stitches are looser.

It is inevitable, as a beginner, that you will drop stitches; even experts cannot fully avoid this mistake. However, mistakes are as easy to fix as they are to make. Keep a small crochet hook with you as you knit, and hook each missed strand through the loop of the dropped stitch.

Retrieving a dropped stitch using needles

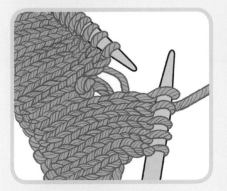

1 This shows what a dropped stitch looks like. If left, it will drop further to form a ladder. If this occurs, you must pick up each strand of the ladder, lowest first, to account for each row.

2 First, slip the dropped stitch loop onto the left needle. Pick up the strand of yarn from the ladder with right-hand needle.

3 Slip the dropped loop from the left needle onto the right needle. Finally, slip the strand of yarn over the loop and off the end of the right-hand needle, as if binding off. Continue in this way until all the strands are picked up, from top to bottom.

Finishing

The finishing of a garment is often something that knitters dread. Good finishing is not even noticeable when the garment is complete, but bad finishing is glaringly obvious. However, if you learn to do it correctly, finishing can be very satisfying.

Selvedge edges

Every piece of knitted fabric has what is called a "selvedge edge," an edge formed as the work progresses. Every flat piece of knitting has selvedges on where the fabric has been cast on, on the right and left edges, and on the cast-off edge. Round knitting has only cast-on and cast-off selvedges. Just as gauge is important during knitting stitches, it is also important that the gauge is correct when selvedge edges are formed. Pulling too tight or not enough when forming an edge will cause problems later when making up the garment, pulling it out of shape.

Finishing touches

Collars, pockets, and buttonholes are all "finishing touches." Pockets are usually knitted into a garment, but they can also be attached later on by sewing as a patch. They are a practical addition to an item of clothing and are inserted horizontally or vertically, as part of the fabric. They will use extra yarn, so buy more than you need—there is nothing worse than running out of yarn just before you finish a project.

There are three main forms of pocket: inserted vertical pockets, patch pockets, patch pockets with a flap.

Neckbands and collars can be various shapes and styles, making use of different hem stitches. On any garment where it has been worked as part of the main fabric, the neck opening will require neatening by the addition of a neckband or collar. The standard method for doing this is to pick up the required number of stitches round the neck opening and work a few rows in a single or double rib. The aim is to form a neat edge which is elastic enough to hold its shape when the garment is pull over the head.

When adding a collar to a jersey or cardigan, either pick up stitches round the neck edge or make a separate section and sew this round the neck edge.

Neat hems and waistbands are very important, particularly on smaller garments such as those knitted for babies or children, where any unnecessary bulk will produce unsightly or uncomfortable edging. Different hem stitches are described on pages 216–218.

Selvedge edge.

Weaving in ends

Never cut the loose ends of yarn left at the edges of your knitting less than 4–8 in (10–20 cm) long, as these can slip through the loops of the stitches easily and unravel. However, these ends need to be tidied.

There are many ways of doing this by threading the ends in and out of the stitches on the reverse side of the work in any way that makes the length become invisible. This can be achieved by hooking the yarn through with a small crochet hook, or weaving in and out using a large tapestry needle. This needle needs to be blunt in order to ensure the point only passes through the stitches and not the actual yarn, which can become messy.

Weaving in ends

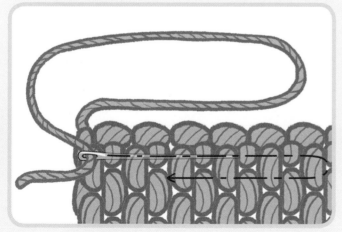

1 Thread the yarn through the loops along the edge of the work for around 1½–2 in (4–5 cm), then sew back through a few of the last loops to secure.

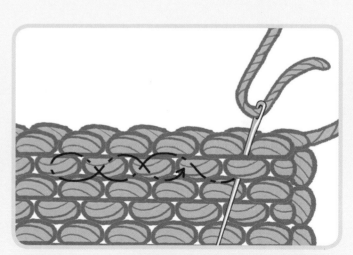

2 Pass the end through the stitches, inserting the needle from the top of the loop on the first, then the bottom on the next alternately for about 1½–2 in (4–5 cm), then sew back through a few of the last loops to secure.

Invisible seams

Bad finishing can be really noticeable in seams; therefore, a mattress stitch, sewn with a blunt tapestry needle, is the best way to make them. In a stockinette stitch or ribbed fabric this is invisible if executed correctly.

With right sides of both pieces of fabric toward you, secure yarn at the bottom of one piece. Pass needle to other section and pick up one stitch, which you can see on the needle in this picture. Pull yarn through and pull tightly. Insert needle through one stitch of first section, entering where the yarn exited previously. Continue in this way, from one side to the other, as if lacing a corset, until you reach the last stitch, secure tightly. If you have entered through the right section as shown above, the seam will be virtually indistinguishable from rest of fabric.

Always be sure to use the same color of yarn as in the main body of work (here it is just to highlight the technique) so that when the seams are pulled and moved when worn, the joining yarn cannot be seen. Some yarns may be too weak or fancy to sew along a seam, so double these up, add a stronger yarn to the original, or use a different yarn, but ensure it is the same color.

Tip

It is better to use a separate piece of yarn to sew seams rather than the tail left over from casting on. If you do make a mistake, it can easily be pulled out of the fabric rather than having to unpick it.

Grafting

Grafting the toe in a sock is the original use for this technique, but it is fabulous for many different seams. The shoulder seam worked in short rows lends itself well to grafting, but any two pieces of knitting that have been left on the needles rather than cast off can be grafted together using "Kitchener stitch" or grafting for an invisible seam.

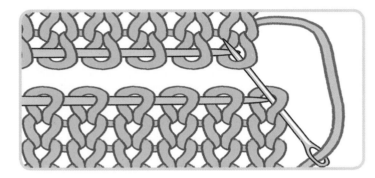

1 Using the knitting yarn, work from right to left. From the back of the fabric, bring the needle through the first knitted stitch of the lower fabric, and through the first stitch of the upper fabric.

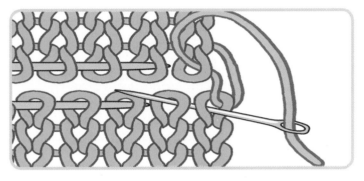

2 From the front, thread the needle back through the center of the first stitch on the lower fabric where the yarn leaves, then out of the center of the next stitch on the left.

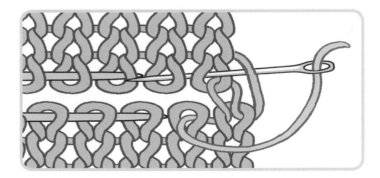

3 Thread the needle through the center of the top stitch and along the center of the next. Continue like this and, as each stitch is worked, keep slipping the knitting needle from them.

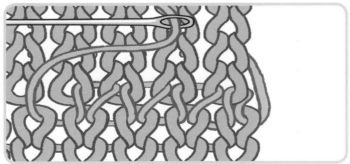

4 Continue like this.

Picking up stitches

Most knitted pieces have an edging or border of some kind to neaten the edge and prevent the fabric from curling. While lace edgings and tassel-type edgings are generally sewn onto the piece, ribs and bands tend to be worked by picking up stitches.

Stitches must be picked up evenly; if too few stitches are used, the knitted piece will pucker, and if too many are picked up, the band will flare. Stitches are picked up either through the whole or half of the edge stitch, using a knitting needle or crochet hook.

Marking the edge for picking up stitches
Measure the edge of the knitted piece and place large-ended pins, or markers, at even intervals—for example, every 2 in (5 cm).

To calculate how many stitches to pick up between the markers, divide the number of stitches required by the number of sections.

Picking up stitches along a horizontal edge
Around a neckline or on a blanket or throw, you need to pick up along a bound-off edge. This is done using one needle, and with the right side facing you.

Picking up stitches along a horizontal edge

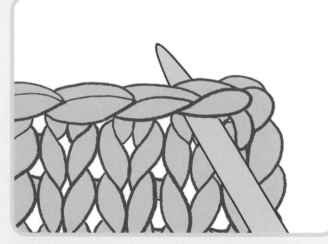

1 Hold the needle in your right hand and insert it through the center of the first stitch below the bind-off from front to back.

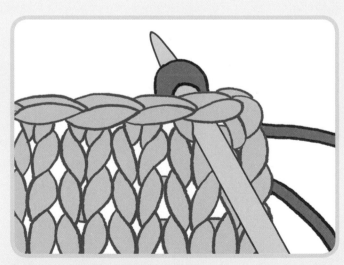

2 Wrap a new piece of yarn around the knitting needle from back to front, as if to knit.

Picking up stitches along a vertical edge

A vertical pickup is done one stitch in from the edge of the knitted piece, using one needle and with the right side of the work facing you. However, because a knitted stitch is not symmetrical and there are more rows than stitches to most knitted gauges, you do not need to pick up on every stitch.

Picking up stitches along a vertical edge

1 Insert the knitting needle between the first and second stitches at the bottom corner of the knitted piece.

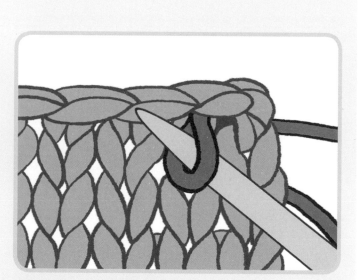

3 Pull the loop through the knitted stitch to the front.

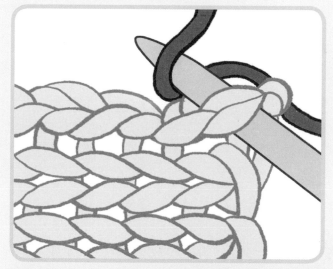

2 Wrap the yarn around the knitting needle from back to front and pull the loop through the knitted piece.

Buttonholes

Buttonholes can be worked quite easily within knitting, by casting off a certain number of stitches on one row, then casting them on again in the next, or simply by placing an eyelet (see Increasing, page 56). The eyelet buttonhole is common in baby's garments as it is fairly small, but if repeated throughout the work it can also be used to make lace patterns. Eyelets are easy to create but look pretty and complicated.

Eyelet buttonhole

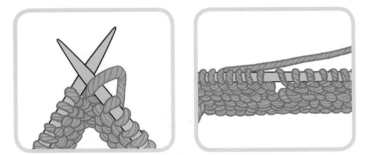

Knit to position of eyelet hole, bring yarn forward (yfwd) to front of work in between needles, just as you would if you were going to purl the next stitch, but instead knit the following 2 stitches together (k2tog). This decrease of one stitch cancels out the increase made by bringing the yarn forward, so that you only have a hole and not extra stitches. On the next row, knit yarn forward loop as if it were a normal stitch. Hole made.

Horizontal buttonhole

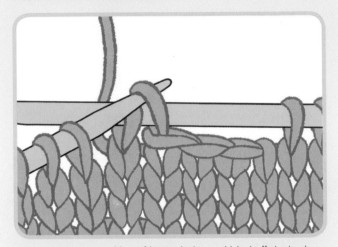

1 Knit across to position of buttonhole, and bind off desired number of stitches according to width of hole needed to fit button. Continue knitting to end of row.

2 Knit across to position of buttonhole and first bound-off stitch, cast on same amount of stitches as were bound off on previous row, across the hole made; pick up stitches on other side of hole and knit to end of row. Buttonhole complete.

Vertical buttonhole

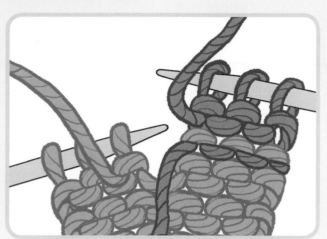

1 Knit across to position of buttonhole, turn and leave rem sts unworked either on holder or on the needle. Work on these sts for desired length of buttonhole, then leave these sts on holder, and rejoin yarn to unworked sts on first holder.

2 Work these sts until same length of fabric worked as to first side of buttonhole. Work 1 row across these sts and those left on second holder to complete buttonhole.

Circular knitting

Circular knitting, or knitting in the round, is a term used to describe a method of knitting that creates a seamless fabric. The method can be worked on circular needles or on a set of four or five double-pointed needles.

When doing stockinette stitch in the round, you never need to purl—you can just knit every row without turning, as you are effectively always on the same side of the knitting. However, this means that to do garter stitch (usually knit every row), you will need to alternate between knit and purl rows.

There are many advantages to working with sets of four double-pointed needles or a pair of circular needles, and they are especially useful when using the Fair Isle technique or working neckbands or cuffs. The only technique that cannot be worked in the round is intarsia.

As with all knitting, work a swatch to judge the gauge, as this can change when you are using a combination of knit and purl rows. However, do remember if you are working stockinette that the gauge will be different from usual, as you will never have to do a purl row when working in the round—usually this purl row can differ greatly in gauge. Therefore, you need to do your gauge swatch in the round, too.

Circular needles

Make sure the circular needle you choose is long enough to hold the number of stitches in the pattern. However, remember that if the length of needle is too long, the stitches won't stretch all the way around the cord to complete a round unless you use the magic loop (see page 71). Cast on the stitches and spread them along the length of the circular needle, making sure that the row is not twisted. Mark the first stitch with a contrast thread or stitch marker to keep track of the beginning of the round.

You can still create a flat piece of knitting using knit and purl rows using circular needles, which is great when knitting while traveling, or if you are prone to losing needles. Simply turn the work at the end of every row and swap needles between hands.

Double-pointed needles

Double-pointed needles, or dpns, are available in sets of four or five. Divide the stitches evenly between three or four of the needles and, once the cast-on row has been made, use the fourth/fifth needle to knit. Once all the stitches from one needle have been knitted onto the fourth, use the free needle to work the stitches along from the next needle. Keep the gauge of the stitches constant when transferring from one needle to another; always draw the yarn up firmly when knitting the first stitch at the changeover point to avoid a ladder or loopy stitch. As with circular needles, ensure the cast-on row is not twisted before you start knitting and use a stitch marker to identify the first stitch.

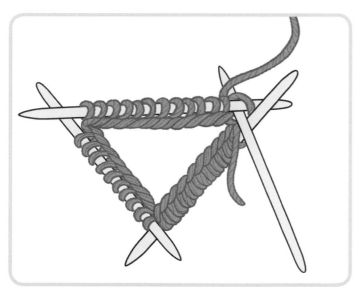

The magic loop

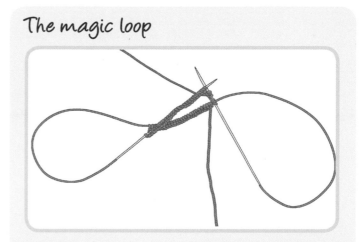

This technique can be used on smallish sets of stitches if you find double-pointed needles daunting, or if you want to use just one needle all the way up a project that decreases in stitches, such as a hat.

You will need a very long needle—at least 30 in (80 cm), but preferably 39 in (1 m) circular or longer if possible.

Cast on the stitches and divide them in half equally, placing half on one needle and the rest on the cord. Pull a length of the cord through the gap between the two sets of stitches. Make sure that the row is not twisted. Join for working in the round by placing a marker for the first stitch of the round, then pull the right-hand needle slightly out of its stitches, while leaving the other half of the stitches on the left-hand needle. Knit the stitches from the left-hand needle normally, using the right-hand needle, pulling tightly on the yarn for the first couple of stitches to ensure the round joins seamlessly.

The right-hand needle will now have stitches on it, and the left-hand needle will not. Therefore, you need to pull the cord so that the stitches on it are on the left-hand needle and then pull out the right-hand needle, leaving its stitches on the cord, so you can use it to knit off the left-hand needle. Continue in this way for the required length of fabric.

Examples of decorative eyelet hole lace patterns.

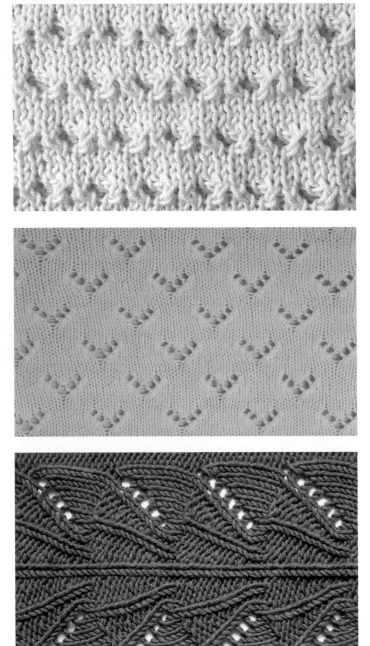

Lace stitches

At its simplest, lace knitting is making planned, secure holes at regular intervals to form shaped patterns.

Lace knitting is basically a series of eyelet holes (see Increasing, page 56, and Buttonholes, page 62) arranged to create a pattern, but with each eyelet, which is in effect an increase, there is a corresponding decrease to ensure that the pattern keeps a constant number of stitches. The pattern or chart for the lace piece will always show you where to increase and decrease so you don't need to worry about this.

Charts

Lace knit patterns, especially more complex ones, are often written as charts, and these are easy to follow when you know how. When you knit from a chart, start at the bottom right-hand corner and work upward. Follow the first row from right to left—just as you make the stitches onto the right-hand needle. You then follow the chart in a zigzag, following the next row from left to right. This is because at the second row, you turn the knitting around.

A plus point to following charts as opposed to written instructions is that they can often show the pattern you are trying to knit more clearly, as you can see the basic outline of your pattern as it will finally look, rather than just looking at a jumble of letters.

Each square is a stitch, and before you start knitting, you should familiarize yourself with the symbols used.

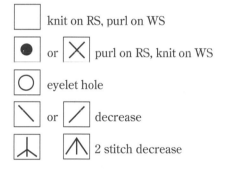

knit on RS, purl on WS

● or ✕ purl on RS, knit on WS

○ eyelet hole

＼ or ／ decrease

⋏ ⋀ 2 stitch decrease

Lifelines

As some lace patterns can be very complicated, it is easy to make mistakes. The trouble with making mistakes in lace is that, due to all the increasing and decreasing, it can be nearly impossible to unpick the stitches without dropping a few or varying the correct stitch pattern. Therefore, it can be helpful to thread a long length of slightly finer, contrast color of yarn through an entire row every so often—perhaps the first or last row of every pattern repeat—then if a mistake is made, you can pick back safely to the so-called "lifeline" without dropping any stitches, safe in the knowledge that the pattern will still be correct as the thread will be keeping all the stitches from that row in the correct place.

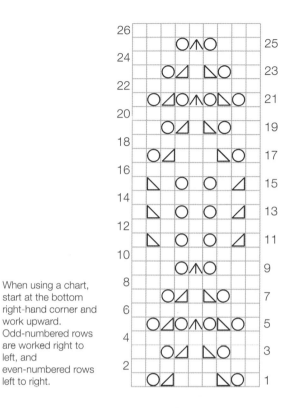

When using a chart, start at the bottom right-hand corner and work upward. Odd-numbered rows are worked right to left, and even-numbered rows left to right.

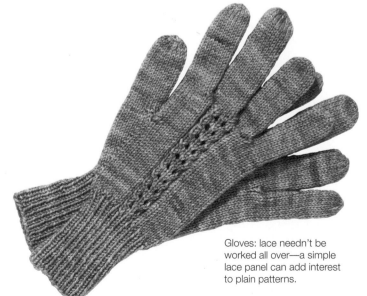

Gloves: lace needn't be worked all over—a simple lace panel can add interest to plain patterns.

Aran knitting

Aran knitting is a style that typically uses lots of cables and other embellishments. Cables are groups of stitches that look like twisted ropes and plaits. These look very complicated but are actually quite simple to do. Making a cable merely involves working stitches, or group of stitches, out of sequence.

For example, instead of working the sequence 1, 2, 3, 4, a cable would work in the order 3, 4, 1, 2. In order to do this, a cable needle (a short, double-pointed needle) is used to hold the first stitch(es) to the front or back while the stitch(es) that follow are worked. The knitting is then resumed from the cable needle.

Whether the stitches held on the cable needle are placed at the front or the back of the work determines the direction of the twist—to the left or to the right. If they are at the front, the twist will be left-leaning, or an "s" twist; if held at the back, it will lbe right-leaning, or a "z" twist. If you hold the cable needle in the same place all the way up the cable—for example, you always hold the stitches to the back—you will get a twisted rope effect, whereas if you change the direction each time, alternating between the front and back, you will end up with a snakelike wiggle, lying on top of your fabric.

All cable crossings will be done on the right side and therefore, there will always be an odd number of rows in between each twist. The remaining stitches in an ordinary Aran pattern will follow the established pattern. In other words, the cable stitches will be knit on the right side and purl on the wrong side, while the stitches next to them will be purl on the right side and knit on the wrong side. After you have done a couple of pattern repeats you should learn the pattern by heart.

Cable needles are best in plastic, not metal, as the plastic grips the stitches better, meaning the cable needle is less likely to slip out. You can also get kinked cable needles designed to prevent slipping. They are available in different diameters and lengths and conform to the standard knitting-needle size guides although, provided you do not stretch the stitches, you do not have to use the same size needle as you used to knit, as the cable needle just holds the stitches and doesn't form them. Cables are usually worked in stockinette stitch on a plain or ribbed ground, with one or two purl stitches either side to allow them to stand out.

As well as raising the surface, cables contract the knitted fabric, so it is usually a good idea to work increases into the base of a cable panel or motif and decreases into the top to prevent flaring below and above.

Cable graphs

You can follow a cable pattern either with abbreviations, as for a normal knitting pattern, or with a graph or chart, as for lace. Cable charts are read in the same way as lace charts, but use some different symbols:

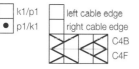

k1/p1	left cable edge	
p1/k1	right cable edge	
		C4B
		C4F

The crossed cable symbol will be drawn across the amount of stitches you need to work the cable across; here it is 4 but if it were 8 stitches, the symbol would cross over 8 squares.

Bobbles

Bobbles can be worked individually or all over a fabric, and are often used among cables in Aran knitting. Methods for making them can vary, but basically a bobble is usually made when lots of stitches are created from one stitch in a cluster. Exact details of how to work the bobble (how many stitches to increase by and how many rows to knit) will always be included in the abbreviations in the pattern.

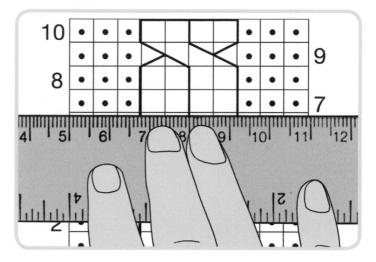

It can be helpful to move a piece of paper, post it, or ruler up the chart as you work each row to track your progress without confusion.

Examples of simple cables worked over a ground of rib.

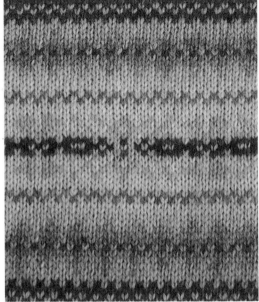

Examples of intricate colorwork Fair Isle patterns.

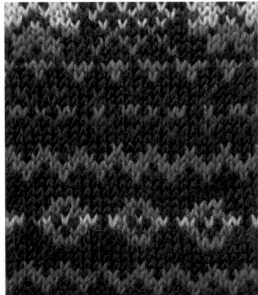

Colorwork

There are two main ways to create different-colored designs within a knitted piece. In Fair Isle knitting, small areas of color are created, only ever using two colors per row, with yarns carried across the back of the work to create a double weight of fabric. In intarsia, areas of color are created using separate ends of yarn. This method produces a single weight of fabric in which many colors can be used on a single row.

Fair Isle

Fair Isle is one of the most isolated of the Shetland Islands in Scotland, on the same latitude as Greenland. Over the centuries the islanders have evolved a knitting method in which, when one color is in use, the others are neatly woven into the back of the knitting.

Fair Isle is most effective when worked on stockinette stitch, although introducing purl stitches can look effective and adds a little texture to the knitted piece.

Before you start on a garment or other knitted project involving Fair Isle, it is very important that you knit up a gauge sample. Fair Isle tends to create a slightly bulky fabric, and if the yarns are carried across the back too tightly, the piece will start to pucker.

Fair Isle can be worked by holding the yarn in either one or two hands. The basic technique is called "stranding."

The very familiar rose motif is used frequently in Fair Isle and colorwork patterns from around Northern Europe.

Colored knitting in the round

Variations of the Fair Isle technique cropped up all over northern Europe. The Norwegians, for instance, invented multicolored knitting in the round, worked on circular needles or sets of double-pointed needles, creating a tubular piece of knitted fabric that was then cut to incorporate sleeves and the neckline. Compared to working on two needles, this is a very quick way of working, which eliminates the use of purl rows. The idea of cutting into your lovingly knitted fabric might seem abhorrent, but knitting, especially wool, is surprisingly resilient, particularly with this method, in which so-called "steeks" are knitted. This means you should not experience the horrors of dropped stitches and raveling. In fact, this way of knitting is extremely economical, resulting in little wasted time, yarn, and effort.

Stranding

Stranding is where a color that is not being used is carried across the back of the work across the other color, without being caught in with that other color. When done properly, there should be no tangling of yarns across the row or round.

It is best to leave not more than three (although up to five is manageable) stitches between a change in color, since the yarn can create loops, called "floats," on the reverse of the fabric which get caught or snagged when the piece is in use.

Stranding one-handed on knit rows or rounds

Stranding with one hand, if you knit the English way (see page 36), involves dropping one yarn after use, then picking up another from underneath and carrying it across the back of the work. It is important not to twist the yarns in the changeover between the colors. When using the continental method of knitting you place both colors on your index finger. The main color should always be closest to your knitting and the contrast next to it. Try to keep their position constant to avoid unnecessary twisting.

Stranding two-handed on knit rows or rounds

If you knit the English way, using the stranding technique with two hands is faster than using just one since the yarns do not need to be dropped between color changes. Hold one color over the forefinger of the left hand and the other according to the style in which you knit in the right hand.

When the stranded technique has been worked correctly, the carried yarn sits horizontally over stitches on the reverse side of the work.

Stranding one-handed on knit rows or rounds

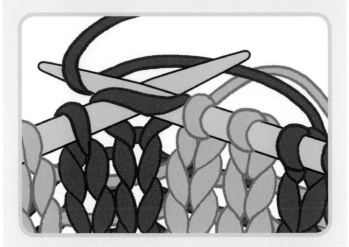

On a right-side (knit) row: using the main color knit the desired number of stitches. Drop MC. Using your right hand, bring the second color from underneath, across the back of the work, over the top of the first yarn, and knit the next stitches. Be careful not to pull the yarn too tightly when you use the main color after knitting several stitches with the contrast yarn.

Stranding two-handed on knit rows or rounds

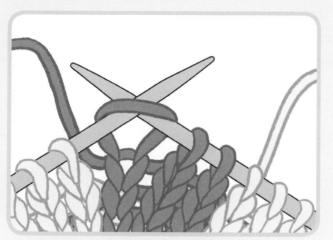

1 On a right-side (knit) row, using the main color and the continental method, knit three stitches.

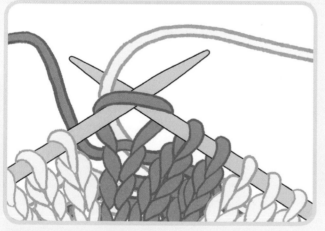

2 Using your right hand, bring the second color across the back of the work, over the top of the first yarn, and knit the next three stitches. Be careful not to pull the yarn too tightly when you use the main color after knitting several stitches with the contrast yarn.

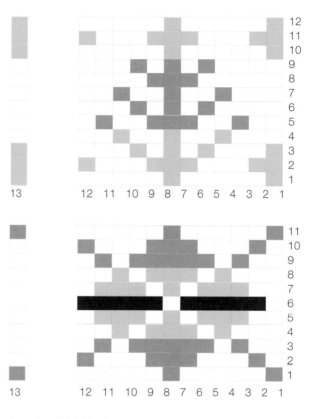

Examples of Fair Isle charts

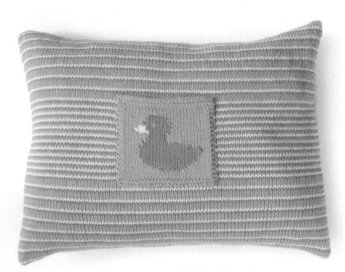

Intarsia

The intarsia method creates separate areas of color within the knitted piece. A separate length of yarn is used for each section of colored knitting, and the yarns are twisted where they meet to create a single piece.

Intarsia is best worked over stockinette stitch, although areas of more textural stitching such as garter stitch and moss stitch can also look very effective when used in conjunction with intarsia.

Before you settle down to work, read through the pattern carefully and check how much yarn you need in each color. To work intarsia effectively you will need to learn a few basic techniques: bobbin winding, joining in new colors, and changing from one color to another on both a knit and a purl row.

Bobbins

Bobbins are used when you do not wish to have a whole ball of yarn attached to the knitted piece while working intarsia. Bobbins can be bought ready-made with the yarn wrapped around them, or you can make your own. For larger areas of color you may wish to wrap the yarn in small plastic bags, secured with rubber bands.

To make your own bobbin

1 Wrap the yarn around the thumb and finger of your right hand in the form of a figure-eight.

2 Carefully remove the yarn from your fingers and cut it from the ball. Wind the loose end of yarn around the center of the figure-eight and secure it tightly.

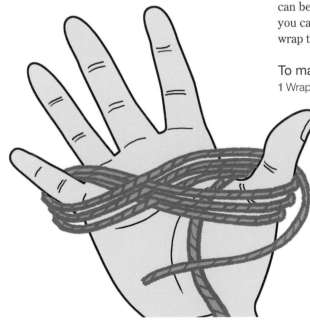

When using a bobbin, pull the yarn from the center a little at a time and keep it as close to the work as possible to avoid tangling.

Joining in a new color

You may find that a new color of yarn is needed across a row of stitches, or that an existing bobbin is running out. In these cases you will need to join in a new color.

1 Insert the right-hand needle into the next stitch. Place the yarn over the working yarn and between the two needles, with the tail end to the left side.

2 Bring the new yarn up from under the existing yarn and knit, dropping both yarns from the left needle after you have done so.

Changing colors

When working an intarsia design, colored areas of stitching are worked from separate balls. If these areas are not joined together in some way, you will end up with individual pieces of color with large gaps in between. Simply cross the yarns to ensure that the knitting stays as one piece.

Changing color on a knit row: Work to the point where you need to change color. Insert the right-hand needle into the next stitch knitwise. Take the first color over the top of the second color and drop. Pick up the second color, ensuring that the yarns remain twisted, and continue according to the pattern.

Changing color on a purl row: Work to the point where you need to change color. Insert the right-hand needle into the next stitch purlwise. Take the first color over the top of the second color and drop. Pick up the second color, ensuring that the yarns remain twisted, and continue according to the pattern.

Reading a graph

All intarsia and most Fair Isle patterns are set out in the form of a graph. Graphs are read as for lace and cable charts (see pages 73 and 75)—from bottom to top, read from right to left on a knit row, and from left to right on a purl row (if you knit in rows). When knitting in the round, read graphs from bottom to top, from right to left on each row of the graph.

Most patterns are now printed in color, but those printed in black and white will have a key to one side describing what colors are placed where, with each color represented by a symbol.

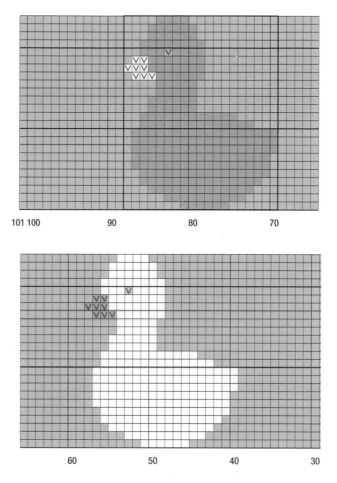

It is a good idea to photocopy the pattern, so that you can mark off rows as you knit without ruining your master copy, or use a ruler to mark the row you are on. Photocopying is also useful if the graph is small, as you can enlarge it to a more readable size.

Projects

The following patterns are all designed with the aim of gradually building up a knitter's skill level, moving on from simple projects, to intermediate ones and then gradually introducing the advanced techniques. The techniques used are all introduced in the guide at the beginning of the book, so all the knowledge you will need to knit them, you will find within the pages of this book.

Each pattern also gives tips for adapting the pattern slightly and suggests yarn alternatives if you don't like or can't find the yarn used in the original design. This means that you are gradually building up knowledge of yarn weights and confidence in your knitting ability.

Simple Projects

Simple garter stitch scarf 86

Fingerless gloves 88

Beanie hat 90

Striped pillow 92

Over-the-shoulder bag 94

Patchwork blanket 96

Slash-neck sweater 98

Simple shrug 102

Dotty cowl 104

Seed stitch beret 106

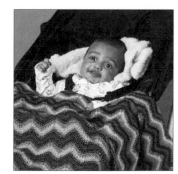

Chevron blanket 108

Simple crew-neck sweater 110

Intermediate Projects

Double-breasted cardigan 114

Mittens in the round 118

Round-yoke cardigan 122

Ankle socks 126

Ribbed sweater 130

Felted bag 134

Basic lace scarf 136

Cabled hat in the round 138

Fair Isle mittens 140

Intarsia pillow 144

Cabled hottie 148

Aran sweater tunic 150

Advanced Projects

Lacy socks 156

Fair Isle yoke sweater 160

Lace panel gloves 164

Fair Isle cardigan coat 170

Lace stole 174

Cabled afghan 178

Simple garter stitch scarf

A simple garter stitch scarf is the perfect project to begin with when knitting, as you have no shaping or tricky techniques to master and you can perfect your gauge while simply knitting every row. If you don't want to try striping too soon, then simply make a plain colored scarf first.

 Yarn
- Artesano Aran, 50% superfine alpaca/50% Peruvian highland wool, 7 oz (100 g), 144 yd (132 m)
- 1 ball each of:
  Shade 2184, Meadle Shade c969, Ash

 Measurements
- One size. Scarf measures approx 7 in (18 cm) wide and 50 in (127 cm) long

Gauge
- Approx 17 sts and 30 rows to 4 in (10 cm) over garter st using size 8 (5 mm) needles or size required to obtain correct gauge

Notions
- Size 8 (5 mm) needles
- Tapestry needle

Instructions

Using either yarn and size 8 (5 mm) needles, cast on 30 sts.

Work in garter stitch (knit every row) for entire scarf, changing color every 2 rows until scarf is desired length or the yarn runs out.

Weave in all ends and block lightly.

 Yarn alternatives
Use any worsted-weight yarn to achieve the same size scarf, or try different yarns; the resulting scarf will just come out smaller or larger. Try scraps of yarn from your stash or left over from other patterns in this book for a colorful and textural project.

Fingerless gloves

Such a simple idea—no shaping required! The ribs cling to the contours of the hands and arms, and the knitting is just a simple rectangle, sewn into shape with a hole left for the thumb. You can vary the length, from cropped gloves to elegant "armwarmers," depending on your mood—simply knit more or fewer rows.

Yarn
- Blue Sky Alpacas, Alpaca Sportweight, 100% baby alpaca, 3½ oz (50 g), 110 yd (100 m)
- 2 skeins 220 yd (200 m) of shade 521, Tangerine

Measurements
- One size—rib will stretch to accommodate most female and male hand sizes. Finished (unstretched) size approx 10 in (25 cm) long and 2¾ in (7 cm) wide

Gauge
- Approx 33 sts and 30 rows to 4 in (10 cm) over rib pattern (unstretched) using size 3 (3.25 mm) needles or size required to obtain correct gauge

Notions
- Size 3 (3.25 mm) needles
- Tapestry needle

Yarn alternatives
The principle of sewing up ribbed rectangles can work for any weight of yarn—simply change the number of stitches you cast on accordingly.

Instructions (makes two)

Using size 3 (3.25mm) needles, cast on 47 sts.

Row 1(RS): k2, (p2, k3) to end of row.
Row 2: (p3, k2) to last 2 sts, p2.
Rep these two rows until gloves measure 10 in (25 cm) or desired length.
Bind off all stitches in pattern, loosely.

Finishing

Fold rectangle in half, with WS together and sew up neatly from bottom in matress st for 5½ in (14 cm). Leave a gap of 2½ in (6 cm) for thumb and sew up rem 2 in (5 cm) in neat mattress st.

Beanie hat

This is a very basic pattern with sizes for all the family. Change the stitch at the brim or add stripes for fun variations.

Yarn
- Rowan Felted Tweed Aran, 50% merino wool/25% alpaca/25% viscose, 3½ oz (50 g), 95 yd/87 m

Measurements
- Head size

in	14	15¼	17¾	19½	21½	23½
cm	35	39	45	50	55	60
balls	1	1	2	2	2	

2Gauge
- Approx 17 sts and 22 rows to 4 in (10 cm) over St st using size 7 (4.5 mm) needles or size required to obtain correct gauge

Notions
- Size 7 (4.5 mm) needles
- Tapestry needle

Yarn alternatives
Any Aran or worsted-weight yarn will substitute, or try cotton for a spring-weight baby hat.

Instructions

Using size 7 (4.5 mm) needles, cast on 61(67:79:85:97:105) sts. Now choose whether you want a garter stitch edge or a ribbed edge and follow corresponding instructions for brim.

Garter stitch brim
Knit 6 rows in garter stitch.
Now follow instructions for main section.

Ribbed brim
Work 6 rows in 1x1 rib as folls:
Row 1(RS): k1, (p1, k1) to end of row.
Row 2: p1 (k1, p1) to end of row.
Rep these two rows for rib.
Now follow instructions for main section.

Main section of hat
Work straight in St st for 4(4¼:4¾:5:5½:6) in/10 (11:12:13:14:15) cm, beg with a k row and ending with a p row.

Shape crown
Row 1: [k8(9:11:12:10:11), k2tog] to last st, k1. 55(61:73:79:89:97) sts.
Row 2 (and every other row): purl.
Row 3: [k7(8:10:11:9:10), k2tog] to last st, k1. 49(55:67:73:81:89) sts.
Row 5: [k6(7:9:10:8:9), k2tog] to last st, k1. 43(49:61:67:73:81) sts.
Row 7: [k5(6:8:9:7:8), k2tog] to last st, k1. 37(43:55:61:65:73) sts.
Continue in this way, working one less st between each decrease on every other row until you have 13(13:13:13:17:17) sts.

Do not bind off, but fasten off yarn and thread through rem sts. Pull up to form ring, then sew up side seam neatly with mattress stitch.

Block lightly to shape.

Simple Projects

Striped pillow

If you are bored of scarves and yet not brave enough to try more complex items just yet, then a pillow is the prefect project for you. It is simply a square of knitting, folded around a pillow form.

Yarn

- Colinette Art, 71% wool, 29% bamboo, 100g, 189 yd (173 cm)
- 1 each of Vincent's Apron, Pierro, Castagna, Velvet

Measurements

- One size—to fit pillow approx 14 x 14 in (35 x 35 cm)

Gauge

- Approx 18 sts and 30 rows to 4 in (10 cm) over garter st using size 8 (5 mm) needles or size required to obtain correct gauge

Notions

- Size 8 (5 mm) needles
- Tapestry needle
- Pillow form
- 3 large buttons, approx 1 in (2.5 cm) diameter

Instructions

Pillow

Using any yarn, cast on 56 sts and work straight in garter st in stripes of two or four rows of color, alternating between all colors as desired until work measures approx 28 in (72 cm), or until piece of knitting is long enough to wrap around the pillow form with some overlap. Note that the first row is the right side of the fabric.

Bind off all sts.

Finishing

Fold knitting around pillow so that overlapping section is apparently a third of the way down back of pillow. Sew up two side seams neatly with mattress st.

Leave overlapping flaps open, to remove pillow for washing. Make 3 I-cords (see page 219) approximately 3½ in (9 cm) long using yarn C. Attach along the edge at back of pillow at regular intervals and sew buttons to corresponding place on back of pillow to fasten.

Yarn alternatives

Any Aran or worsted-weight yarn substitutes here, but you can try other yarn types, too; you will simply have to buy a smaller or larger pillow form depending on the size of the knitting. The amounts of yarn used here will allow you to make a few pillows to create a stunning set.

Over-the-shoulder bag

This is a very basic but useful bag pattern. Make sure you line the bag and strap to ensure that the knitting doesn't stretch.

Yarn
- Rowan Silk Twist, 53% silk/30% wool/12% superkid mohair/5% polyamide, 3½ oz (50 g), 93 yd (85 m)
- 2 balls of shade 670, Navy

Measurements
- Pouch measures approximately 7 in (18 cm) wide and 6¼ in (16 cm) high
- Bag hangs approximately 21 in (53 cm) long

Gauge
- Approximately 20 sts to 4 in (10 cm) over woven pattern using size 7 (4.5 mm) needles or size required to obtain correct gauge

Notions
- 1 pair size 7 (4.5 mm) needles
- Fabric for lining
- 6 in (0.5 cm) narrow ribbon
- Large button
- Tapestry needle

Instructions

Woven pattern
Row 1 (RS): knit.
Row 2: knit.
Row 3: p1, (k1, p1) to end of row.
Row 4: k1, (p1, k1) to end of row.
Rep last four rows for pattern.

Front
Using size 7 (4.5 mm) needles, cast on 35 sts and work in woven stitch for 6¼ in (16 cm), ending with a row 2.
Next row: (k2tog) to last st, k1. 18 sts.
Bind off all sts.

Back
Using size 7 (4.5 mm) needles, cast on 35 sts and work in woven stitch for 6¼ in (16 cm), ending with a row 2.
Next row: (k2tog) to last 3 sts, k3tog. 17 sts.
Next row: knit.
Cont in woven st, beg with a row 3, for a further 2½ in (6 cm), ending with a row 2.
Bind off all sts.

Yarn alternatives
Worsted-weight yarn will substitute here. Choose a yarn with some silk or sparkle to achieve a sheen.

Strap/sides

Using size 7 (4.5 mm) needles, cast on 10 sts and work in garter stitch for approx 45 in (114 cm).
Bind off all sts.

Finishing

Cut three pieces of fabric, one for each knitted piece, making each piece of fabric approximately ½ in (1 cm) bigger than the knitted fabric all around for a hem. Line all pieces of bag with fabric, neatly sewing fabric onto reverse of pieces with whipstitch. Sew cast-on and bound-off edges of strap together, making sure you do not twist the strap. With all fabric sides facing inward, sew sides of strap to front and back pieces of bag, placing strap seam at bottom center of bag and sewing around bottom and side front and back pieces. Cut ribbon and sew ends together to form a loop. Position loop on WS of back flap. Sew on securely to form button fasten. Sew a button to front of bag.

Simple Projects

Patchwork blanket

A blanket made of square swatches is the perfect way to practice new stitches without feeling you are wasting time and yarn. Simply knit as many as you wish and sew them together—it couldn't be easier!

Yarn
- King Cole Merino Blend Aran, 100% pure new wool superwash, 3½ oz (50 g), 88 yd (80 m)
- Approximately 4 balls each of:
  shade 780, Sage
  shade 772, Rose
  shade 774, Terracotta
  shade 783, Lavender

Measurements
- Each square measures approximately 4 x 4 in (10 x 10 cm) and the blanket uses 36 squares

Gauge
- Each square will differ slightly in gauge depending on the stitch used, but will be approximately 18 sts and 24 rows to 4 in (10 cm) over st st using size 7 (5 mm) needles

Notions
- 1 pair size 7 (5 mm) needles
- Tapestry needle

Instructions

Use the stitch directory on pages 180–219 to choose a range of stitches to practice.

Using size 8 (5 mm) needles and any shade of yarn, cast on around 20 sts (or closest relevant multiple if using stitch guide) and work in chosen stitch pattern until square measures approx 4 in (10 cm). Bind off all stitches in pattern.

Make as many squares as you wish for preferred size of blanket in same way.

Finishing
Lay out all squares into desired blanket formation and sew together neatly either using mattress stitch or, if you wish the join to become a feature, blanket stitch or another fancy stitch in a contrasting shade of yarn.

Yarn alternatives
Any worsted-weight yarn will produce the same size blanket, but you can use any weight of yarn and the blanket will simply knit up a different size. This is a perfect project for scraps, and you can even use different weights of yarn for each square for a really textural end result.

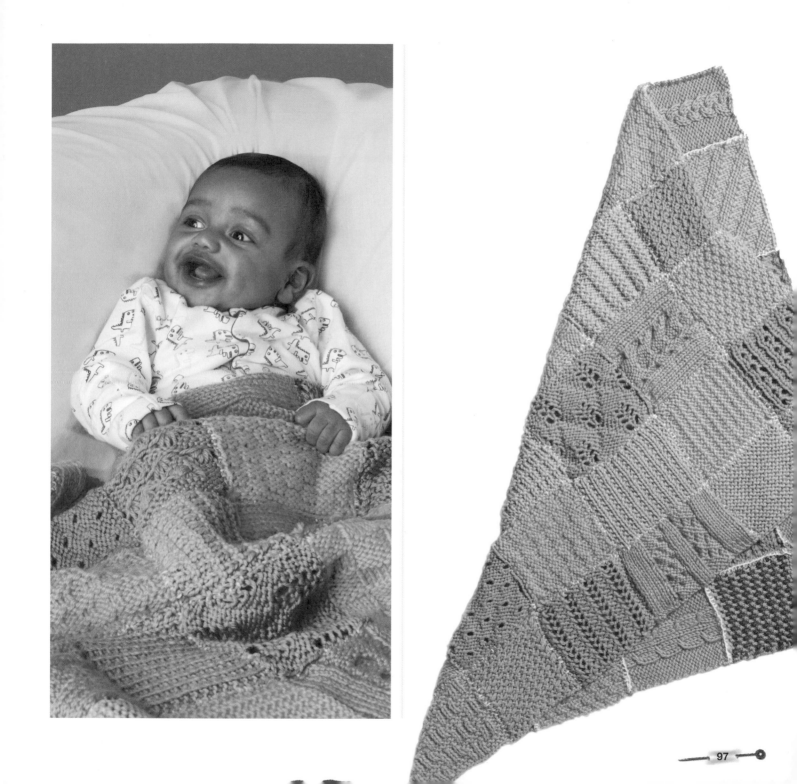

Simple Projects

Slash-neck sweater

The garter stitch used in this sweater means that knitted-on edges are not required to neaten the cuffs or neckline, making it an incredibly simple sweater to knit for any little one—the perfect pattern for a first garment attempt.

Yarn
- Madeline Tosh Vintage, 100% Superwash merino wool, 110g, 200 yd (182 m)
- 3(4:5) skeins of Wood Violet

Measurements

	Child (S)	Child (M)	Child (L)
To fit chest			
in	21¾	24	25¾
cm	55	60	65
Actual size			
in	24	25¾	27½
cm	60	65	70
Length			
in	12½	14¼	16
cm	32	36	40
Sleeve seam			
in	11	12	13
cm	27	30	33

Gauge
- Approx 20 sts and 25 rows to 4 in (10 cm) over St st using a size 7 (4.5 mm) needle

Notions
- 1 pair size 7 (4.5 mm) needles
- Tapestry needle
- 6 buttons approx ½ in (1 cm) in diameter

Instructions

Note
Sweater worked all in one piece, front first, increasing out for the arms, then worked over to the back, leaving a hole for the neck. Fold piece in half and sew up underarm seams to complete.

Front
Using size 7 (4.5 mm) needles, cast on 62(68:74) sts and work approx 1 in (3 cm) straight in garter stitch (knit every row).

Change to stockinette stitch and work straight until front measures 6½(8:9) in/16(20:23) cm from cast-on, ending with a p row.

Change back to working in garter stitch and increase 55(61:67) sts at beg of next 2 rows for sleeves.

Cont on these 172(190:208) sts until work measures 12(13½:16) in/30(34:40) cm from cast-on edge, ending with an RSR.
Next row: k67(75:83), bind off next 38(40:42) sts, k to end.
Work straight on k67(75:83) sts for right sleeve for ¾ in/2 cm, ending with a WSR.

Place these stitches on a holder and rejoin yarn to left sleeve and work straight for ¾ in/2 cm, ending with an RSR. Cast on 38(40:42) sts, knit k67(75:83) sts from holder for right sleeve.

Back
Cont on these 172(190:208) sts for back in garter stitch until back

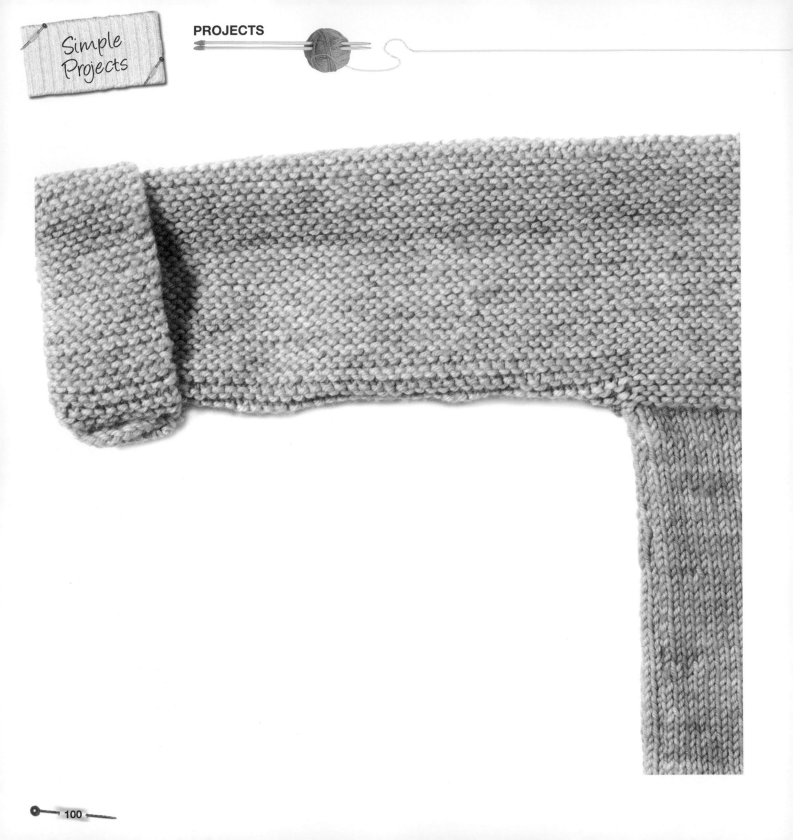

Back

Cont on these 172(190:208) sts for back in garter stitch until back measures 6½(6½:6¾) in/16(16:17) cm from neck.

Change to stockinette stitch and work straight until back measures 11½(13:14½) in/29(33:37) cm from neck.

Change to garter st and work 1 in (3 cm) in garter st.

Finishing

Sew up side and underarm seam of either side in one go.

Yarn alternatives

This yarn is perfect for children and babies as it is soft merino wool and yet can be machine-washed. Substitute any worsted-weight yarn that has just these properties.

PROJECTS

Simple shrug

The easiest way to make a basic cover-up is to knit a long rectangle and fold it in half, sewing along the armhole seams. That is all there is to this piece! You can also increase the amount you knit to make the sleeves longer.

Yarn

- Orkney Angora St Magnus 50/50 DK, 50% angora/50% lambswool, 3½ oz (50 g), 218 yd (200 m)
- 3 balls of shade 03, Heather

Measurements

- Length approx

	XS	S	M	L	XL
	16¾	17½	18	19¼	30¾ in
	42.5	44	46	49	52.5 cm

Gauge

- 24 sts and 30 rows to 4 in (10 cm) over St st using size 7 (4.5 mm) needles or size required to obtain correct gauge

Notions

- Pair each of size 4 (3.5 mm) and size 7 (4.5 mm) needles
- Tapestry needle

Instructions

Using size 4 (3.5 mm) needles, cast on 51(53:55:59:63) sts and work 11 in (28 cm) in 1x1 rib as folls:

Row 1 (RS): k1, [p1, k1] to end of row.

Row 2: p1 [k1, p1] to end of row.

Rep last two rows for desired length of rib, ending with a row 2.

Change to larger needles.

Next row: knit twice into every stitch. 102(106: 110:118:126) sts. Work 25½ in (65 cm) in rev St st on these sts, beg with a p row and ending with a p row.

NB: if you wish the shrug to be longer, for a custom fit, continue knitting to desired length, minus 11 in (28 cm) for final ribbed cuff, then finish rem cuff as normal.

Next row: (k2tog) across row. 51(51:55:59:63) sts.

Change to smaller needles and work in 1x1 rib as before for 11 in (28 cm) beg with a row 1.

Bind off all sts in pattern.

Yarn alternatives

Any DK or light worsted yarn will work here to achieve the same gauge. If you do not like the hairiness of angora, try pure lambswool.

Finishing

Fold shrug in half widthwise, with wrong sides together (this pattern uses reverse St st as the correct side, but you can use normal St st as the right side if you wish).

Sew up one ribbed cuff seam neatly with mattress st, continuing to sew seam up the rev St st section for approx 4 in (10 cm).
Leave center section unsewn, then sew up rem ribbed cuff in same way.

This particular yarn is quite weak for sewing up, so you may need to hold it double or use an alternative matching shade of yarn for sewing up.

Dotty cowl

An excellent way to practice working in the round, this simple cowl is a basic tube and can easily be made wider or longer by casting on extra stitches or working extra rows. It utilizes the very pretty dot stitch with a seed stitch border to prevent curling edges.

Yarn
- King Cole Baby Alpaca DK, 100% pure baby alpaca, 3½ oz (50 g), 110 yd (100 m)
- 2 balls of shade 509, Plum

Measurements
- One size, approx 6¼ in (16 cm) wide and 24½ in (62 cm) circumference

Gauge
- Approx 20 sts and 28 rows to 4 in (10 cm) over dot stitch using size 7 (4.5 mm) needles or size required to obtain correct gauge

Notions
- Size 7 (4.5 mm) 24-in (60-cm) long circular needle
- Stitch marker
- Tapestry needle

Yarn alternatives
Any DK or light worsted yarn will substitute, but the cowl can easily be made in any weight of yarn—the result will simply be a differently sized cowl.

Instructions (makes two)

Dot pattern
Rnd 1: k1, (p1, k3) to last 3 sts, p1, k2.
Rnd 2: knit.
Rnd 3: (k3, p1) to last 4 sts, k3, p1.
Rnd 4: knit.
Rep these 4 rnds for pattern.

Cowl
Using size 7 (4.5 mm) needle, cast on 124 sts (or a multiple of four if you wish to make it wider) and join for working in the round, being careful not to twist the work, placing a marker at the end of rnd. Do not turn throughout.
Rnd 1: (k1, p1) to end of rnd.
Rnd 2: (p1, k1) to end of rnd.
Rep these two rows twice more.

Begin working in dot pattern until approx 5½ in (14 cm) from cast-on edge or desired length minus ¾ in (2 cm) for rem seed st band.
Next rnd: (k1, p1) to end of rnd.
Next rnd: (p1, k1) to end of rnd.
Rep last two rows twice more.

Bind off all sts in pattern loosely, weave in ends, and block lightly to shape.

Seed stitch beret

Hats are always more fun in the round—they seem to fly off the needles and it is near impossible to put them down. This is a pretty and fun pattern to try for one of your first projects in the round.

Yarn
- Rennie Handknits Supersoft 4–ply Lambswool, 3½ oz (50 g), 270 yd (246 m)
- 2 balls of shade 1484, Raspberry

Measurements
- To fit adult woman's head size

cm	52(S)	54(M)	56(L)
in	20½	21¼	22

band unstretched is approx

cm	50	52	54
in	19½	20½	21¼

Gauge
- 26 sts and 38 rows to 4 in (10 cm) over St st using 1 strand of yarn and size 2 (3 mm) needles; 20 sts and 24 rows to 4 in (10 cm) over seed st using 2 strands of yarn held together and size 6 (4 mm) needles, or size required to obtain correct gauge

Notions
- size 2 (3 mm) 16–in (40–cm) long circular needle
- size 6 (4 mm) 16–in (40–cm) long circular needle
- size 6 (4 mm) double-pointed needles
- Tapestry needle
- Stitch marker

Instructions

Using size 2 (3 mm) circular needle, and 1 strand of yarn, cast on 130(134:140) sts and join for working in the rnd, placing marker at beg of rnd. Work 10 rnds St st (knit every row in the round), then purl 1 row for hemline, work a further 10 rnds St st (knit every row).

Change to size 6 (4 mm) circular needle, and two strands of yarn held together. Inc rnd: k4(0:0), inc in first st, [k4(3:3), inc in next st] to last 5(5:3) sts, k4(4:2), inc in next st. 156(168:176) sts.
Work in seed st for 5(5½:6) in/13(14:15) cm as folls:
Rnd 1: [k1, p1] to end of rnd.
Rnd 2: [p1, k1] to end of rnd.
Rep last 2 rnds for seed st, ending with a rnd 2 for sizes S and L, end with a rnd 1 for size M.

Decrease for crown as folls:

Sizes S and L only
Rnd 1: *k1, [p1, k1] 9 times, p3tog, rep from * to last 2(0) sts, k2(0). 142(160) sts.
Rnd 2 (and every other rnd): [p1, k1] to end of rnd.
Rnd 3: *k1, [p1, k1] 8 times, p3tog, rep from * to last 2(0) sts, k2(0). 128(144) sts.
Continue in this way, working two sts less in between each decrease until there are 16 sts left, changing to DPNs when it is no longer comfortable to use circular needles.

Size M only

Rnd 1: *[p1, k1] 9 times, p3tog, rep from * to end of rnd. 152 sts.
Rnd 2 (and every other rnd): [k1, p1] to end of rnd.
Rnd 3: *[p1, k1] 8 times, p3tog, rep from * to end of rnd. 136 sts.
Continue in this way, working two sts less in between each decrease until there are 24 sts left, changing to DPNs when it is no longer comfortable to use circular needles.

All sizes

Break yarn and thread through rem sts, pull up tight to close ring, and secure.
Fold back rim seam along purl row and hem up along the cast-on edge.
Block lightly to shape, using a dinner plate to retain circular shape if you wish.

Yarn alternatives
Any fine, 4–ply, or sockweight yarn will substitute here.

Chevron blanket

A bright and cheerful chevron stripe can make a relatively simple knit fantastically striking. Use as many different colored yarns as you dare, or just use two—whatever you do is sure to produce a fabulous blanket.

Yarn
- Debbie Bliss Andes, 65% baby alpaca/35% mulberry silk, 3½ oz (50 g), 109 yd (100 m)
- For multicolored blanket:
  4 skeins each of:
  - Yarn A: shade 004, Brown
  - Yarn B: shade 007, Peach
  - Yarn C: shade 010, Lime
  - Yarn D: shade 009, Green
  - Yarn E: shade 012, Blue
  - Yarn F: shade 013, Purple
  - Yarn G: shade 015, Pink
- For blue and white blanket
  8 skeins each of
  - Yarn A: shade 012 Blue
  - Yarn B: shade 007, Cream

Measurements
- One size, approx 39 x 59 in (100 x 150 cm)

Gauge
- Approx 26 sts and 25 rows to 4 in (10 cm) over chevron st using size 7 (4.5 mm) needles or size required to obtain correct gauge

Notions
- Size 7 (4.5 mm) needles
- Tapestry needle

Instructions

Chevron Pattern
Row 1 (WS): k3, p to last 3 sts, k3.
Row 2: k4, inc into next st, k4, sl1, k1, psso, k2tog, k4, *inc into each of next 2 sts, k4, sl1, k1, psso, k2tog, k4; rep from *to last 5 sts, inc into next st, k4.
Row 3: k3, p to last 3 sts, k3.
Row 4: Repeat row 2.
These 4 rows form pattern, rep for length of fabric.

Multicolored blanket
With color A, cast on 258 sts.
Work in chevron pattern, changing color every two rows in alternate stripes of yarn A to G until desired length is work.
Bind off all sts.

Blue and white blanket
With color A, cast on 258 sts
Rows 1–2: Cream
Rows 3–4: Blue
Repeat last 4 rows five times more
Rows 25–28: Cream
Rows 29–30: Blue
Repeat last 6 rows five times more
Rows 61–62: Cream

Yarn alternatives
Any weight of yarn can be substituted here and the blanket will simply come out larger or smaller.

Rows 63–64: Blue
Repeat last 4 rows once more
Rows 69–70: Cream
Rows 71–74: Blue
Rows 75–78: Cream
Repeat last 8 rows twice more
Rows 95–132: Blue
Repeat rows 59–70 once more
Rows 133–144: repeat rows 59–70 once more
Rows 145–148: Blue
Rows 149–150: White
Repeat last 6 rows five times more
Bind off all sts.

These 180 rows form the pattern repeat for the length of blanket.

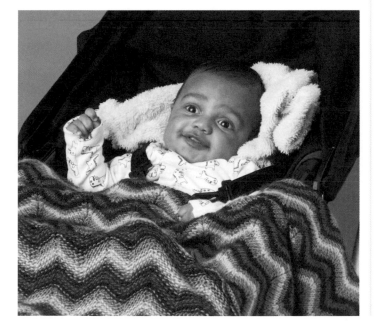

Simple crew-neck sweater

This sweater introduces picking up stitches for a neckline as well as setting in sleeves. The variations in stitches show how you can easily adapt a pattern to fit in a stitch that you adore.

Yarn

BABY SIZE
- Debbie Bliss Baby Cashmerino, 55% merino wool/33% microfiber/12% cashmere 3½ oz (50 g), 136 yd (125 m)
- 3(5:6:7) balls of shade 003, Mint

ADULT SIZE
- Cascades 220 Sport, 100% Peruvian highland wool, 3½ oz (50 g), 164 yd (150 m)
- 9(9:10:11:12:13) balls of shade 8400, Gray

Gauge
- Approx 24 sts and 32 rows to 4 in (10 cm) over St st using a size 5 (3.75 mm) needle; approx 24 sts and 30 rows to 4 in (10 cm) over basket weave using a size 5 (3.75 mm) needle

Notions
- Pair each of size 5 (3.75 mm) and size 4 (3.5 mm) needles
- Tapestry needle
- Stitch holders

Yarn alternatives
You can interchange yarns for your projects using yardage as a guide. Use a sportweight yarn, and stick to washable yarns for the baby and child sizes.

Instructions

Note
Child and female sizes are stockinette stitch. Adult male sizes can be worked in either St st or basketweave pattern. Basketweave worked over a multiple of 12 sts: plus 6 (adult sizes). The gauge is the same for both baby and adult sizes.

Basketweave pattern
Back
Row 1: (k6,p6) to last 6 sts, k6.
Row 2: (p6,k6) to last 6 sts, p6.
Row 3–8: rep rows 1–2 three times.
Row 9: rep row 2.
Row 10: rep row 1.
Rows 11–16: rep rows 9–10 three times.

Front
Row 1: (p6,k6) to last 6 sts, p6.
Row 2: (k6,p6) to last 6 sts, k6.
Rows 3–8: rep rows 1–2 three times.
Row 9: rep row 2.
Row 10: rep row 1.
Rows 11–16: rep rows 9–10 three times.

Pattern starts
Back
Using size 4 (3.5 mm) needles, cast on 61(77:81:85:109:113:121:125:137:149) sts and work in 1 x 1 rib for 3 in (8 cm), increasing 1 st at end of last row. 62(78:82:86:110:114:122:126:138:150) sts.
Change to larger needle and work in either stockinette stitch or basket weave until back measures 12(13:14:15¾:21¾:22½:23¾:25½:26½:27¼) in/30(33:35:40:55:57:60:65:67:69) cm long, ending with a WS row.

Measurements

BABY SIZE	XS	S	M	L
To fit chest				
in	18	22	24	26
cm	46	56	61	66
Actual size				
in	20	25½	26¾	28
cm	51	65	68	71
Length				
in	12	13	14	15¾
cm	30	33	35	40
Sleeve seam				
in	8¼	11½	12¼	13
cm	21	29	31	33

ADULT FEMALE	S	M	L
To fit chest			
in	33	35	37
cm	84	89	94
Actual size			
in	36	37½	39¾
cm	91	95	101
Length			
in	21½	22½	23½
cm	55	57	60
Sleeve seam			
in	19	19¾	21
cm	48	50	54

ADULT MALE	S	M	L
To fit chest			
in	39	42	46
cm	99	107	117
Actual size			
in	41½	45¼	49¼
cm	105	115	125
Length			
in	25½	26½	27¼
cm	65	67	69
Sleeve seam			
in	22	23	23¾
cm	56	58	60

Bind off 17(23:25:26:35:35:38:38:43:47) sts, patt across 28(32:32:34:40:44:46:50:52:56) sts, place these 28(32:32:34:40:44:46:50:52:56) sts on a holder for back, bind off rem sts.

Front

Using size 4 (3.5 mm) needles, cast on 61(77:81:85:109:113:121:125: 137:149) sts and work in 1 x 1 rib for 3 in (8 cm), increasing 1 st at end of last row. 62(78:82:86:110:114:122:126:138:150) sts.

Change to larger needles and work in either stockinette stitch or basket weave until back measures 10(11:12:13¼:19¼:20:21¼:23:23¾:24½) in/ 25(28:30:34:49:51:54:58:60:62) cm long, ending with a WS row.

Next row: patt across 40(50:52:55:69:72:76:78:86:94) sts, place last 18(22:22:24:28:30:30:30:34:38) sts onto a holder, patt to end.

Cont on these 22(28:30:31:41:42:46:48:52:56) sts for right neck as folls:

Child and adult female sizes only
Row 1: patt to end.

Adult male sizes only
Row 1: patt to end, dec 1 st at end of row.
Row 2: bind off 3 sts, patt to end.
Row 3: patt to end, dec 1 st at end of row.

All sizes
Cont in pattern for right neck, decreasing 1 st at neck edge of next and every following RS row until 17(23:25:26:35:35:38:38:43:47) sts rem.

Work straight on these sts until front measures the same as back, ending with a WS row.

Bind off all sts.

Rejoin yarn to left neck and work to match right side, reversing all shaping.

Sleeves

Using size 4 (3.5 mm) needles, cast on 33(37:39:43:49:53:57:59:63:69) sts and work 1¼(1¼:1½:2:2½:2¾:3:3:3:3) /3(3:4:5:6:7:8:8:8:8) cm 1 x 1 rib.

Child sizes only
Change to larger needles and work in st st, increasing 1 st at both ends of next and every foll 3rd(4th:4th:4th) row until 71(79:81:85) sts.

All adult sizes only
Change to larger needles and work in st st, increasing 1 st at both ends of 5th and every foll 6th row until 93(97:103:109:115:123) sts.

All sizes
Cont working straight until sleeve measures 8¼(11½ :12¼:13:19:19½: 21¼:22:22¾:23¾)in/21(29:31:33:48:50:54:56:58:60) cm long.

Bind off all sts.

Finishing

Seam together left shoulder seam, then pick up stitches for neck as follows:

Using smaller needles, with RSF, attach yarn to back neck and work across k28(32:32:34:40:44:46:50:52:56) sts on holder for back neck, pick up and knit 12(12:12:14:14:14:14:16:16:17) sts down left front, knit 18(22:22:24:28:30:30:30:34:38) sts from holder for front neck and pick up and knit 12(12:12:14:14:14:14:16:16:17) sts up right front. 70(78:78: 86:96:102:104:112:118:128) sts.

Work on these sts in 1 x 1 rib for 4 rows.

Bind off loosely in rib.

Seam up rem shoulder and neck seam, set in sleeves, and then sew up side seam and underarm seam in one go, either side.

Double-breasted cardigan

A fabulously classic and practical little number, this cardigan uses the pretty seed stitch border for a little bit of texture and to create a flat front.

Yarn
- Malabrigo Twist, 100% baby merino wool, 7 oz (100 g), 150 yd (137 m)
- 7(8:9:10) skeins of shade 076, Manzanilla Olive

Measurements
ADULT FEMALE

	S	M	L
To fit chest			
in	32–34	36–38	40–42
cm	81–86	91–97	112–117
Actual size			
in	35	39	43
cm	90	100	110
Length			
in	21½	22½	23½
cm	54	56	59
Sleeve seam			
in	12½	13½	14
cm	32	34	36

Gauge
- 17 sts and 22 rows to 4 in (10 cm)

Notions
- 1 pair each of size 9 (5.5 mm) and size 8 (5 mm) needles
- 6 buttons, approximately ½ in (1.5 cm) diameter
- Sewing needle and matching thread
- Tapestry needle

Instructions

Seed stitch
Row 1 (RS): k1, (p1, k1) to end of row.
Rep row 1 for pattern.

Important
When working in seed st, be careful when decreasing—make sure you continue in correct seed st pattern; you may not begin every row with a knit depending on how many you have decreased.

Back
Using smaller needles, cast on 78(86:94:102) sts and work in 2 x 2 rib for 3 in (8 cm) as folls:
Row 1: k2, (p2, k2) to end of row.
Row 2: p2, (k2, p2) to end of row.
Rep last 2 rows for pattern, ending with a row 2.

Change to larger needles and work straight in St st beg with a k row until work measures 14(14¼:15:15½) in/35(36:38:39) cm, ending with a p row.

Shape armholes
Bind off 5 sts at beg of next 2 rows, then dec 1 st at both ends of next 4(4:6:8) rows. 60(68:72:76) sts.

Now decrease 1 st at both ends of every alternate RS row until 54(60:64:68) sts rem.

Work straight in St st until work measures 7½(8:8¼:9) in/19(20:21:23) cm from armhole shaping, ending with a p row.

Bind off 6(7:7:8) sts at beg of next 4 rows, leave rem 30(32:36:36) sts on holder for back neck.

Left front panel

Using larger needles, cast on 17 sts and work straight in seed st until panel measures approx 10(10¼:11:11¼) in/25(26:28:29) cm, ending with an RSR.

Next row (WS): dec 1 st at beg of row (neck edge), cont in seed st to end of row.

Now cont in seed st, dec 1 st at neck edge of 4(5:7:7) foll rows, then every foll alt row 7 times, then every foll third row until no sts rem.

Right front panel

Using larger needles, cast on 17 sts and work straight in seed st for two rows.

Buttonhole row 1: patt 2 sts, bind off 2sts, pattern 8 sts, bind off 2 sts, patt to end.
Buttonhole row 2: patt 3 sts, cast on 2 sts, patt 8 sts, cast on 2 sts, patt to end.

Cont straight in seed st, working a buttonhole as before after 4½(5:5½:5¾) in/11.5(13:14:14.5) cm and after 9½(10:10¾:11) in/24(25:27:28) cm, then work straight until panel measures approx 10(10¼:11:11¼) in/25(26:28:29) cm, ending with a WSR.

Next row (RS): dec 1 st at beg of row (neck edge), cont in seed st to end of row.

Now cont in seed st, dec 1 st at neck edge of 4(5:7:7) foll rows, then every foll alt row 7 times, then every foll third row until no sts rem.

Fasten off yarn.

Left front

Using smaller needles, cast on 30(34:38:42) sts and work in 2 x 2 rib for 3 in (8 cm) as folls:
Row 1: k2, (p2, k2) to end of row.
Row 2: p2, (k2, p2) to end of row.
Rep last 2 rows for pattern, ending with a row 2.

Now cont straight in st st, beg with a k row until work measures same as back to armhole shaping, ending with a WSR.

Bind off 5 sts at beg of next row, then dec 1 st at armhole edge of next 4(4:6:8) rows.

Now dec one st at armhole edge of every alt row 3(4:4:4) more times.

At the same time, when the left front is the same as left front panel to top of shaping, then dec 1 st at neck edge of every foll 3rd row 0(0:3:1) times, then every foll 4th row until 12(14:14:16) sts rem.

Work straight on these 12(14:14:16) sts until front measures same as back to shoulder, ending with a WSR.

Bind off 6(7:7:8) sts at beg of next row.

Work one row straight, then bind off rem sts at beg of next row.

Right front

Work as for left front, reversing all shaping.

Sleeves

Using smaller needles, cast on 44(52:60:64) sts and work in 2 x 2 rib for 3 in (8 cm) as folls:

Row 1: k2, (p2, k2) to end of row.
Row 2: p2, (k2, p2) to end of row.
Rep last 2 rows for pattern, ending with a row 2.

Change to larger needles and work straight in St st beg with a k row until work measures 12½(13¼:14:15) in/32(34:36:38) cm, ending with a p row.

Shape armholes

Bind off 5 sts at beg of next 2 rows, then dec 1 st at both ends of next 3(4:6:6) rows. 28(34:38:40) sts.

Now decrease 1 st at both ends of every alternate RS row until 16(18:22:26) sts rem. Cont straight in St st until work measures approx 4¾(5:5½:6) in/12(13:14:15) cm from armhole shaping, bind off all sts.

Finishing

Join shoulder seams and set in sleeves.

Sew up underarm and side seams with neat mattress st.

Attach front panels to relevant sides of front neatly.

Neck edging

Using smaller needles, and with RSF, pick up and knit 52(54:55:57) sts up right front edge (22 from seed st panel and 30(32:33:35) from St st panel), then knit 30(32:36:36) sts from back neck holder and 52(54:55:57) sts down left front edge (30(32:33:35) sts from St st panel and 22 sts from seed st panel). 134(138:146:150) sts.

Work 4 rows in 2 x 2 rib, then bind off loosely in rib.

Yarn alternatives

Any heavy worsted or chunky weight yarn will work here.

Mittens in the round

This is a great project to practice working in the round—these mittens are so simple that once you've made one pair, you will want to make another in every size!

Yarn

BABY SIZE
- Sublime Baby Cashmere Merino Silk 4–ply, 75% extra fine merino/20% silk/5% cashmere, 3½ oz (50 g), 184 yd (170 m)
- 1 ball each of shade 0051, Clipper (yarn A), and 0100, Paddle (yarn B)

ADULT SIZE
- Sirdar Country Style 4–ply, 45% acrylic/40% nylon/15% wool, 7 oz (100 g), 494 yd (452 m)
- 1 ball of shade 527, Raspberry

Measurements
- Child: approx 5½(6) in/14(15) cm long
- Adult female: approx 8(8½) in/ 20(22) cm long
- Adult male: approx 9½(10¼) in/ 24(26) cm long

Gauge
- Approx 28 sts and 36 rows to 4 in (10 cm) over St st using size 3 (3.25 mm) needles

Notions
- Set of four size 3 (3.25 mm) double-pointed needles
- Set of four size 2 (3 mm) double-pointed needles
- Stitch markers
- Stitch holder or safety pin
- Tapestry needle

Instructions

Note

Smallest child sizes are outside brackets, all other sizes in ascending size order inside brackets. For striped mittens, work pattern in six-row stripes of each color alternately.

It may help to use different colored stitch markers from the beginning of round marker for the placing of the thumb gusset, so you can distinguish one from the other.

Using (size 2) 3 mm needles, cast on 40(44:50:54:58:62) sts and spread across 3 needles for working in the round, placing a marker for beg of round.

Work in 1 x 1 rib for 1½ (1½:2:2½:2¾:2¾) in/4(4:5:6:7:7) cm.

Change to larger needles and st st, increasing 4 sts evenly all round on first row.
Rnd 2: k1, m1, pm, k1, pm, m1, k to end of rnd. 46(50:56:60:64:68) sts.
Rnd 3: knit.
Rnd 4: k to marker, m1, sl marker, k1, slip marker, m1, k to end of rnd, 48(52:58:62:66:70) sts.
Rep last two rnds until there are 56(62:72:78:84:88) sts.
Next rnd: k14(16:20:22:24:24) sts, slip last 13(15:19:21:23:23) sts onto a stitch holder for thumb to work later, k to end of rnd.

Reposition stitches around needles for comfortable working in the round.
Next rnd: inc in first 2 sts, k to last st of rnd, inc in last st. 46(50:56:60:64:68) sts.

Cont on these stitches until mitten measures approx

4¾ (5:6¾:7½:8¼:9) in/12(13:17:19:21:23) cm from cast-on edge, or desired length to tip of fingers, minus ¾(¾:1:1:1¼:1¼)in/ 2(2:2.5:2.5:3:3) cm.

Begin decreasing for top as folls:

Rnd 1: [k4(4:5:5:6:6), k2tog] to last 4(2:0:4:0:4) sts, k4(2:0:4:0:4). 39(42:48:52:56:60) sts.
Rnd 2 (and every other rnd): knit.
Rnd 3: [k3(3:4:4:5:5), k2tog] to last 4(2:0:4:0:4) sts, k4(2:0:4:0:4). 32(34:40:44:48:52) sts.
Rnd 5: [k2(2:3:3:4:4), k2tog] to last 0(2:0:4:0:4) sts, k0(2:0:4:0:4). 24(26:32:36:40:44) sts.
Rnd 7: [k1(1:2:2:3:3), k2tog] to last 0(2:0:0:0:4) sts, k0(2:0:0:0:4). 16(18:24:27:32:36) sts.
Rnd 8: knit.

Child sizes only
Break off yarn and thread through rem 16(18) sts, pull up and tighten to close.

All adult sizes
Rnd 9: k(1:1:2:2), k2tog] to end of rnd. (16:18:24:27) sts.
Rnd 10: knit.

Female sizes only
Break off yarn and thread through rem (16:18) sts, pull up and tighten to close.

Male sizes only
Rnd 11: [k1, k2tog] to end of rnd. (16:18) sts.
Rnd 12: knit.
Break off yarn and thread through rem (16:18) sts, pull up and tighten to close.

Rejoin yarn to 13(15:19:21:23:23) thumb sts and work on these straight until thumb measures approx 1½ (1½:2:2½:2¾:3) in/4(4:5:6:7:8) cm from top of thumb shaping or length desired for thumb, ending with a p row.

Next row: [k2tog] to last st, k1. 7(8:10:11:12:12) sts.
Break off yarn and thread through rem sts, pull up and tighten to close, use rem yarn to sew up thumb seam, and secure hole between thumb gusset and hand.

Weave in all ends and block lightly to shape.

Yarn alternatives
Use any fine, 4-ply or sock weight yarn here. You can work the mittens striped or plain, as shown here.

Round-yoke cardigan

Working garments in one piece means less finishing as there are fewer seams to sew and the shaping often looks much neater, which is great news for anyone who hates sewing up!

Yarn

- Sweet Georgia Superwash Worsted, 100% superwash merino wool, 4 oz (115 g), 200 yd (182 m)
- 5(6:7:8) skeins of shade Savory

Measurements

To fit bust

in	32–34	36–38	40–42	44–46
cm	81–86	91–97	102–107	112–117

Actual size

in	36	40	44	48
cm	92	102	112	122

Length

in	18¾	20	21½	22½
cm	48	52	55	57

Sleeve seam

in	19¾	20	21	22
cm	50	52	54	56

Gauge

- Approx 18.5 sts and 28 rows to 4 in (10cm) over St st using size 7 (4.5 mm) needles

Notions

- Size 7 (4.5 mm) and size 6 (4 mm) 24–31-in (60–80-cm) long circular needles
- Set each of size 7 (4.5 mm) and size 6 (4 mm) double-pointed needles
- Stitch holders
- Stitch markers
- Tapestry needle
- Buttons

Instructions

Special abbreviation: m = marker

Sleeves

Using size 6 (4 mm) dpns, cast on 37[41:45:49] sts and join for working in the round, pm at beg of rnd.

Work in 1 x 1 rib as folls:
Row 1: k1, *p1, k1; rep from * to end of rnd.
Row 1 forms pattern, rep for approx 2 in (5 cm).

Change to size 7 (4.5 mm) dpns and st st.
Inc 1 st at both ends of every following 10th(10th:9th:9th) rnd until 61(67:73:79) sts.
Cont in St st on these sts until work measures 19¾(20:21:22) in/ 50(52:54:56) cm, or desired length to underarm, ending last rnd 4(4:4:5) sts before marker.

Bind off 8(8:8:10) sts and work to end.
Leave these 53(59:65:69) sts on a holder.

Body

For body, you are working straight (backward and forward) on circular needles across all back and fronts sts together, from bottom up.
Using size 6 (4 mm) circular needles, cast on 153(171:189:207) sts and work in 1 x 1 rib as folls:
Row 1 (RS): k1, (p1, k1) to end of row.
Row 2: p1, (k1, p1) to end of row.
Rows 1 and 2: form rib pattern, rep this until rib measures 2 in (5 cm), ending with a row 2, working a buttonhole on row 3 as folls:
Row 3: k1, (p1, k1) to last 4 sts, p1, yo, k2tog, k1.

Change to size 7 (4.5 mm) needles and cont as folls:
Row 1: (k1, p1) twice, place these sts on a holder, k to last 4 sts, place last 4 sts on a holder.
Cont in St st on these 145(163:181:199) sts.
On 4th row, place markers as folls:
Row 4: p18(20:23:25), pm, p36(41:45:50), pm, p37(41:45:49), pm, p36(41:45:50), pm, p to end.
Decrease 4 sts on next row and every foll 4th row until 129(147:165:183) sts rem as folls:
Dec row: (k to next marker, sl m, k2tog, k to 2 sts before next marker, sl1, k1, psso, sl m) twice, k to end.

Work 7(11:15:19) rows straight in St st without decreasing, beg with p row.
Inc 4sts on next and every foll 4th row until 169(187:205:223)sts as folls:
Inc row: (k to marker, sl m, m1, k to marker, m1, sl marker) twice, k to end.

Work straight in St st without shaping until body measures 11(12:12¾:13) in/28(30:32:33) cm from cast-on edge, ending with a p row.

Shape armholes
Next row: k38[43:47:51], cast off 8[8:8:10] sts, k77[85:95:101], cast off 8[8:8:10] sts, sts, k to end.

Yoke
Yoke is worked in garter st.

Next row: k38[43:47:51], k53[59:65:69] sts sleeve stitches from holder with WSF, k77[85:95:101], k53[59:65:69] sleeve stitches from other holder with WSF, work across rem front sts. 259[289:319:341] sts.

Largest size only
On next row, dec 1 st close to an armhole. 340 sts.

All sizes
Cont on these 259(289:319:340) sts in garter stitch until yoke measures 2(2:2¼:2½) in/5(5:5.5:6) cm from armhole, ending with a WSR.

Decrease round.
Next row (RS): (k3, k2tog) to last 4(4:4:0) sts k4(4:4:0).
208(232:256:272) sts.

Work on these sts until yoke measures 4(4¼:4¼:4¾) in/10(11:11:12) cm from armhole ending with a WSR.

Next row (RS): (k2, k2tog) across row. 156(174:192:204) sts.

Work on these sts until yoke measures 6(6¾:6¾:7) in/15(17:17:18) cm from armhole, ending with a WSR.

Next row (RS): (k1, k2tog) across row. 104(116:128:136) sts.

Work on these sts until yoke measures 7¾(8½:9:9¼) in/ 19.5(21.5:22.5:23.5) cm from armhole ending with a WSR.

Work for back neck as folls:

Next row (RS): k78(87:96:102), wrap next st, turn and work 52(58:64:68) sts, wrap next st, turn and work to 4 sts before last left shoulder wrapped st, wrap next st, turn and work to 4 sts before last right shoulder wrapped st, turn and work to end of round.

Work one row.

Last decrease row (RS): (k1, k2tog) across row. 52(58:64:68) sts.

Change to smaller needles and work 4 rows in 1 x 1 rib, increasing one st at end of first row so that each row begs and ends with same sts.

Bind off all sts.

Rejoin yarn to stitches held at front opening of right front and work in 1 x 1 rib on smaller needles until strip is same length as front edge.

Mark placement of desired number of buttons along this edge.

Bind off sts.

Carefully and evenly sew front band to front edge.

Rep for right side edging, placing a buttonhole on an RS row every time you want a button as folls:

Buttonhole row: k1, yo, k2tog, p1.

Sew front edging down and attach buttons to right front band.

Sew up armhole seams and weave in ends.

Block lightly to shape.

Yarn alternatives

Any worsted-weight yarn will substitute here.

Ankle socks

Hand-knitted socks can be fiddly to work at first, but once you have mastered the technique of turning the heel, they can become extremely addictive. This simple pair is a great pattern for your first attempt as the socks are attractive yet surprisingly basic.

Yarn
- Lorna's Laces Shepherd Sock, 80% superwash merino wool/20% nylon, 7 oz (100 g), 435 yd (397 m)
- 1 ball each of:
  Yarn A: shade Poppy
  Yarn B: shade Chino

Measurements
- To fit S(M:L) feet.
  To tailor foot length for a perfect fit, simply keep knitting straight in the round where indicated

Gauge
- 28 sts to 4 in (10 cm) over St st using size 3 (3 mm) needles or size required to obtain correct gauge

Notions
- 1 set each of size 2 (2.75 mm) and size 3 (3.25 mm) double-pointed needles

Yarn alternatives
Any sock-weight yarn will substitute—look for yarns specifically designed for socks as they will be more hardwearing, usually due to their nylon content.

Instructions

Using size 2 (2.5 mm) needles, cast on 56(60:64) sts in yarn A and join for working in the round, placing marker at beg of rnd.
Work 8 rnds in 1 x 1 rib as folls:
Rnd 1: *k1, p1, rep from * to end of rnd.

Rep rnd 1 7 times more.
Change to yarn B and size 3 (3 mm) needles and work 4(4½:4¾) in/ 10(11:12) cm in st st.

Divide for heel
Change to yarn A and knit across 28(30:32) sts. Leave rem 28(30:32) sts on one dpn for instep unknitted.
Work 28(30:32) sts for heel straight on 2 needles as folls:
Row 1: sl1p, p to end.
Row 2: sl1k, k to end.
Rep last 2 rows until you have worked 29(31:33) rows in total from beginning of heel (you will finish on a row 2).

Turn heel
Row 1: k17(17:17), sl 1, k1, psso, k1, turn, leaving rem sts unworked.
Row 2: sl1, p7(5:3), p2tog, p1, turn.
Row 3: sl1, k8(6:4), sl 1, k1, psso, k1, turn.
Row 4: sl1, p9(7:5), p2tog, p1, turn.
Row 5: sl1, k10(8:6), sl 1, k1, psso, k1, turn.
Row 6: sl1, p11(9:7), p2tog, p1, turn.
Row 7: sl1, k12(10:8), sl 1, k1, psso, k1, turn.
Row 8: sl1, p13(11:9), p2tog, p1, turn.
Row 9: sl1, k14(12:10), sl 1, k1, psso, k1, turn.
Row 10: sl1, p15(13:11), p2tog, p1, turn.

Small size only

18 sts rem on needle. Proceed to gusset.

Medium and large sizes

Row 11: sl1, k14(13:12), sl 1, k1, psso, k1, turn.
Row 12: sl1, p15(12:13), p2tog, p1, turn.

Medium size only

18 sts rem on needle. Proceed to gusset.

Large size only

Row 13: sl1, k14, sl 1, k1, psso, k1, turn.
Row 14: sl1, p15, p2tog, p1, turn.
18 sts rem on needle. Proceed to gusset.

Change to yarn B and knit across heel sts with extra dpn for work in the round. With same needle, pick up and knit 14(15:16) sts along side of heel.
Tip: the slipped stitches at the beg of rows when knitting the heel will help you see where to pick up the stitches.

With second dpn, pattern across instep, with 3rd dpn pick up and knit 14(15:16) sts along other side of heel. 74(78:82) sts.
Tip: here it is important to remember that the last st of 3rd needle is last st of rnd.

Knit 1 rnd straight as folls.

Shape instep

Rnd 1: knit to last 3 sts of 1st dpn, k2tog, k1, pattern across all sts of instep on 2nd dpn, on 3rd dpn, k1, sl 1, k1, psso, k to end of needle, k2, p1, (k3, p1) across rest of sts. 72(76:80) sts.
Rnd 2: knit.
Rep last 2 rnds until 56(60:64) sts rem.

Cont on these sts working straight in St st in the round until work measures 5½(6¼:7)in/14(16:18) cm from heel (measure from the darker color of heel), or desired length of foot minus 1 in (3 cm).
Fasten off yarn B.

Shape toe

Change to yarn A.
Rnd 1: knit.
Rnd 2: knit to last 3 sts of 1st dpn, k2tog, k1, on 2nd dpn, k1, sl1, k1, psso, k to last 3 sts on needle, k2tog, k1, on 3rd needle, k1, sl1, k1, psso, k to end of rnd.
Rep last 2 rnds until 28(28:32) sts rem.

The sock is now complete apart from casting off. To save sewing up and bulky toe seams, it is best to close the seam while casting off. To do this, work from the wrong side of the sock as folls.

With wrong side showing, distribute the sts evenly on two dpns, so that the back and front of toe are on separate needles; now bind off using three-needle bind-off (see pages 48–49).

Ribbed sweater

This is a simple pattern yet a very effective stitch; fisherman's rib is a lovely rib as it is especially pronounced.

Yarn
- Lion Brand Superwash Merino Cashmere, 72% superwash merino/15% nylon/13% cashmere, 3½ oz (50 g), 87 yd (80 m)
- 13(13:15:15:17) balls of shade 133, Saffron

Measurements

	xs	s	m	l	xl
To fit chest					
in	32	35	37	39	41
cm	82	89	94	99	104
Actual size					
in	32	35	37	39	41
cm	82	89	94	99	104
Length					
in	20½	21	21¾	22½	23¼
cm	52	53	55	57	59
Sleeve seam					
in	12	12½	13¼	14	15
cm	30	32	34	36	38

Gauge
- Approx 20 sts and 22 rows to 4 in (10 cm) over fisherman's rib pattern.

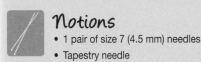

Notions
- 1 pair of size 7 (4.5 mm) needles
- Tapestry needle

Instructions

Special abbreviations
K1b: knit one below = knit into stitch below next stitch.
Sl 1b: slip one below = insert needle into stitch of row below next st as if to knit and slip both loops off needle.
K2togb: knit two together below = work next two stitches together as normal, but insert needle first into stitch below second st, then insert needle as normal through front of next st, finish st k2tog as normal.

Fisherman's rib pattern
Row 1: knit.
Row 2 (RS): k1, (k1b, k1) across row.
Row 3: k1b (k1, k1b) across row.
Rep row 2 and 3 for pattern.

Back
Using size 7 (4.5 mm) needles, cast on 85(89:95:101:105) sts and work 14(14:14½:15:15) in/36(36:37:38:38) cm in fisherman's rib pattern, ending with a row 3.

Shape armholes as follows
Bind off 4(4:4:6:6) sts at beginning of next two rows, then decrease 2 sts at either end of following third row as folls.

Next row: Pattern across three sts, sl 1b, k2togb, pass both loops of sl 1b over, pattern to last 6 sts, sl1b, sl1, sl1b, pass all 5 loops back onto left needle and k3tog (3 sts, 5 loops), pattern to end of row. Decrease as last row on every following 4th row until 61(63:67:71:75) sts rem.

Work straight until back measures 19½(19¾:20½:21:21¾) in/ 49(50:52:53:55) cm, ending with a WSR.

Front

As back.

Sleeves

Using size 7 (4.5 mm) needles, cast on 57(61:65:69:73) sts and work fisherman's rib pattern, increasing 1 st at both ends of 7th(7th:9th :9th:9th) and every foll 8th(8th: 8th:10th:10th) row until there are 73(77:81:85:89) sts, putting each st into fisherman's rib pattern.

Work straight in fisherman's rib until sleeve measures approx 12(12½:13¼:14:15) in/30(32:34:36:38) cm long.

Shape armholes as follows:

Bind off 4 sts at beginning of next two rows, then decrease 2 sts at either end of following third row as folls:

Next row: Pattern across three sts, sl 1b, k2togb, pass both loops of sl 1b over, pattern to last 6 sts, sl 1b, sl1, sl 1b, pass all 5 loops back onto left needle and k3tog (3 sts, 5 loops), pattern to end of row. Decrease as last row on every following 4th row until there are 33(35:37:39:43) sts rem.
Work two further rows, then bind off all sts.

Finishing

Sew up shoulder seams, then set in sleeves.
Sew up side seams and underarm seams in one go.
Weave in all ends.

Shape neck

Pattern across 11(12:13:15:17) sts, bind off next 39(39:41:41:41) sts, patt across rem sts.
Turn and work on these 11(12:13:15:16) sts for left back neck.
Next row: Patt across row, dec 1 st at neck edge.
Cont on these sts, dec 1 st at neck edge of every row until 6(6:7:8:10) sts rem.
Work straight on these sts until back measures 20½(21:21¾:22½:23¼) in/52(53:55:57:59) cm from cast-on edge.
Rejoin yarn to right back neck and complete to match left neck, reversing all shaping.

Yarn alternatives

Any worsted-weight yarn will substitute here.

Felted bag

This is a straightforward pattern for trying out felting your knitting—a felted fabric is perfect for bags as the process strengthens the knitted fabric and reduces the amount of stretch. This means you can carry even your heaviest possessions around without your bag becoming misshapen.

Yarn
- Rowan Big Wool, 100% merino wool, 87 yd (80 m), 7 oz (100 g)
- 1 ball each of:
  Yarn A: shade 049, Lichen
  Yarn B: shade 052, Steel
  Yarn C: shade 059, Oxidised
  Yarn D: shade 058, Heather
  Yarn E: shade 025, Wild Berry

Measurements
- Approximately 19½ in (50 cm) wide at top (fl dt) and 14 in (35 cm) deep

Gauge
- Before felting—approximately 7.5 sts and 9 rows to 4 in (10 cm) using size 17 (12 mm) needles or size required to obtain correct gauge
- After felting—approximately 10 sts and 16 rows to 4 in (10 cm)

Notions
- 1 pair size 17 (12 mm) needles
- Tapestry needle

Yarn alternatives
Any bulky weight yarn that is composed of wool suitable for felting.

Instructions

Stripe pattern
10 rows of each color, alternately from A to E.

Front and back
Using size 17 (12 mm) needles and yarn A, cast on 26 sts.
Work in stockinette stitch, increasing 1 st at both ends of 3rd and every foll 4th row while working stripe pattern.

On row 47, work final increase and hole for handle as folls:
Row 47: inc into first st, k 16, cast (bind) off next 14 sts, k to last st, inc into last st.
Row 48: p to bind off sts, cast on 14 sts, p to end of row.
Row 49: knit across all sts.
Row 50: knit.
Bind off all sts.

Bottom of bag
Using size 17 (12 mm) needles and yarn A, cast on 60 sts.
Row 1: knit.
Row 2 (and every other row): purl.
Row 3: [k4, k2tog] across row. 50 sts.
Row 5: [k3, k2tog] across row. 40 sts.
Row 7: [k2, k2tog] across row. 30 sts.
Row 9: [k1, k2tog] across row. 20 sts.
Row 11: [k2tog] across row. 10 sts.
Break yarn and thread through rem sts and secure into a ring, then sew up side seam to form a circle.

Finishing

Sew up side seams of front and back and sew bottom circle to bottom of front and back evenly.

Tip Don't bother sewing in your ends; you can simply snip these off once the bag is felted.

To felt

Once you have established the temperature and length of cycle in your machine to create the perfect density of felt, pop the finished bag into the machine, preferably with a few other items to aid felting. Once felting is complete, snip off all loose ends and block into shape.

Basic lace scarf

When practicing lace for the first time, try out this very simple allover eyelet pattern so that you can master the art of making holes and decreasing many times without having to follow a complex chart.

Yarn
- Louet Kidlin, 49% linen/35% kid mohair/16% nylon, 3½ oz (50 g), 250 yd (228 m)
- 1 ball of shade 04, Rose Bloom

Measurements
- Approx 9.5 x 60 in (24 x 152 cm)

Gauge
- 18 sts and 22 rows to 4 in (10 cm) over lace pattern

Notions
- 1 pair of size 7 (4.5 mm) needles
- Tapestry needle

Instructions

Lace pattern
Row 1: knit.
Row 2: k1, (yo, k2tog) across row.
Rep last two rows for pattern, ending with a row 1.

Using size 7 (4.5 mm) needles, cast on 45 sts and work in lace pattern until desired length of scarf is reached, ending with a row 1.

Bind off all sts, block lightly to shape, and weave in all ends.

Yarn alternatives
Any light mohair or mohair mix yarn will do here to achieve the same ethereal quality. However you could also try other fibers in anything from a laceweight to a sportweight yarn on larger needles to achieve a pretty lace effect.

Cabled hat in the round

This is a great first project for trying out cables. This hat uses the simplest kind of twisted cable and, as you are working in the round, you are always working on the right side of the fabric, so it is easy to see where you are placing the cables.

 ## Yarn

- O-Wool Legacy Bulky, 100% certified organic merino wool, 7 oz (100 g), 106 yd (97 m)
- 1 ball of shade 6041, Olive

Measurements

- To fit head circumference approx 21¼(23:24½) in/54(58:62) cm

Gauge

- Approx 13 sts and 17 rows to 4 in (10 cm) over St st using size 10 (6 mm) needles
- Approx 14 sts and 19 rows to 4 in (10 cm) over cable pattern using size 10 (6 mm) needles

 ## Notions

- 1 size 10 (6 mm) 16–in (40–cm) long circular needle
- Size 10 (6 mm) double-pointed needles
- Stitch marker
- Cable needle
- Tapestry needle

 ## Yarn alternatives

Any bulky weight will do here—try to pick one with good stitch definition and in a lighter shade so that the cables show up clearly.

Instructions

Note

Special abbreviation: C4F = cable four forward: slip next 2 sts onto cn at front of work, k2, k2 from cn.

Uing circular needle, cast on 66(72:78) sts and join for working in the round, placing marker at beg of rnd.

Work 6 rnds in 1 x 1 rib, then begin cable pattern as folls:

Rnd 1: [k4, p2] across rnd.

Rep last rnd twice more.

Rnd 4: [C4F, p2] across rnd.

Rep last 4 rows until hat measures approx 6¼(7:8) in/16(18:20) cm from cast-on edge, ending with rnd 3.

Change to DPNs.

Decrease for crown

Rnd 1: [k1, k2tog, k1, p2] across rnd.

Rnd 2: [k3, p2] across rnd.

Rnd 3: [sl1, k2tog, psso, p2] across rnd.

Rnd 4: [k1, p2] across rnd.

Rnd 5: [k1, p2tog] across rnd. 22(24:26) sts.

Rnd 6: [k1, p1] across rnd.

Thread yarn through rem sts, then pull up tight to secure hole, and weave in all ends.

Fair Isle mittens

Play around with colors and stripes to make your mittens unique.

Yarn

- JC Rennie Supersoft Cashmere DK, 87.5% lambswool/12.5% cashmere, 3½ oz (50 g), 132 yd (120 m)
- 1 ball each of shades:
  Yarn A: Shade 003, Athena
  Yarn B: shade 044, Enyo
  Yarn C: shade 002, Aphrodite
  Yarn D: shade 046, Lissa
  Yarn E: shade 039, Orion

Measurements

- 9 in (23 cm) long and approx. 7.5 in (19 cm) all round the hand

Gauge

- 24sts and 36sts to 4 in (10 cm) over St st using size 5 (3.75 mm) needles or size needed to obtain correct gauge

Notions

- 1 set each of size 5 (3.75 mm) and size 3 (3.25 mm) double-pointed needles
- Stitch marker
- Stitch holder
- Tapestry needle

Yarn alternatives

Any light worsted or DK weight yarn will substitute here—make sure you use a yarn that will hold together well in the Fair Isle patterning; one with a high wool content is perfect.

Instructions

Work chart from row 1 when indicated, reading chart from right to left every row.

Using smaller needles and yarn A, cast on 40 sts and arrange for working in the rnd, being careful not to twist sts. Work 1½ in (4 cm) in 1 x 1 rib.
Change to larger needles and work in stockinette stitch, increasing 8 sts evenly around first rnd. 48 sts.
Work ½ in (1 cm) in yarn A, then change to yarn B and begin to work in Fair Isle pattern from row 1 until work measures approx 2 in (5 cm) from ribbing, ending last rnd 4 sts before end.
Next row: place next 8 sts on a stitch holder and cast on 8 sts in their place. Rejoin for working in the round and continue in Fair Isle pattern until chart has finished.

Now continue straight in yarn E until mittens measure approx 6 in (15 cm) from ribbing or desired length to end of mitten minus 1 in (2.5 cm).

Decrease for top as folls:
Rnd 1: (k1, k2tog tbl, k19, k2tog) twice. 44 sts.
Rnd 2: (k1, k2tog tbl, k17, k2tog) twice. 40 sts.
Rnd 3: (k1, k2tog tbl, k15, k2tog) twice. 36 sts.
Cont to decrease in this way until 12 sts rem.
Bind off using three-needle bind off, with mitten inside out.
Fasten off yarn.

Rejoin yarn E to thumb stitches on holder, knit across 8 sts, pick up 1 st from side of hole, 8 sts from cast on, 1 st from other side and join these 18 sts for working in the round.
Work straight until thumb measures approx 2½ in (6 cm) or desired length of thumb.
Next row: (k2tog) all round. 9 sts.
Next rnd: knit.
Next rnd: (k2tog) to last st, k1.
Break yarn and thread through rem 5 sts, pull up to close hole, and secure.

Weave in all ends and block lightly to shape.

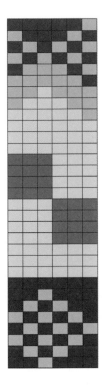

Fair Isle Mittens chart

Intarsia pillow

When trying the intarsia technique for the first time, choose a simple pattern with plenty of plain rows of knitting to make it seem less daunting.

Yarn

- Debbie Bliss Ecobaby, 100% organic cotton 3½ oz (50 g), 137 yd (125 m)
- 3 balls of:
  Yarn A: shade 14005, Blue
- 1 ball of:
  Yarn B: shade 14014, Yellow
  Yarn C: shade 14024, Salmon pink

Measurements

- To fit a pillow form: 12 x 16 in (30 x 40 cm) which may measure 13 x 16 in (32.5 x 40 cm) depending on the manufacturer
- Knitted measurements: 13 x 15 in (32.5 x 38 cm)

Gauge

- 26 sts x 36 rows over 4 in (10 cm) st st using size (3.00 mm) needles or size needed to obtain correct gauge.

Notions

- 1 pair of size 2/3 (3.00 mm) straight needles
- Pillow form 12 x 16 in (30 x 40 cm)
- Tapestry needle

Instructions

Front

Using A, cast on 101 sts and, starting with a knit row, work 12 rows of st st.

Using st st, work from the chart. Knit the beak stitches to be embroidered in duplicate stitch in blue and the eye stitches in the yarn of the surrounding stitches.

**Work 10 rows of st st.

Using the photograph for color reference, work from the chart.

Repeat from ** once more.

Work 12 rows of st st.

Bind off.

Back

Using C, pick up and knit 102 sts along the cast-on edge of the front piece.

Working in st st throughout and starting with a knit row, work the following stripe sequence: B, 1 row; A 3 rows.

Work the following stripe sequence: C, 1 row; B, 1 row; A 3 rows; 7 times.

Work the following stripe sequence: C, 1 row; B, 1 row; A 1 row; 11 times.

Work the following stripe sequence: C, 1 row; B, 1 row; A 3 rows; 8 times.

Work C, 1 row.

Bind off.

Yarn alternatives

Any sport weight yarn will substitute here.

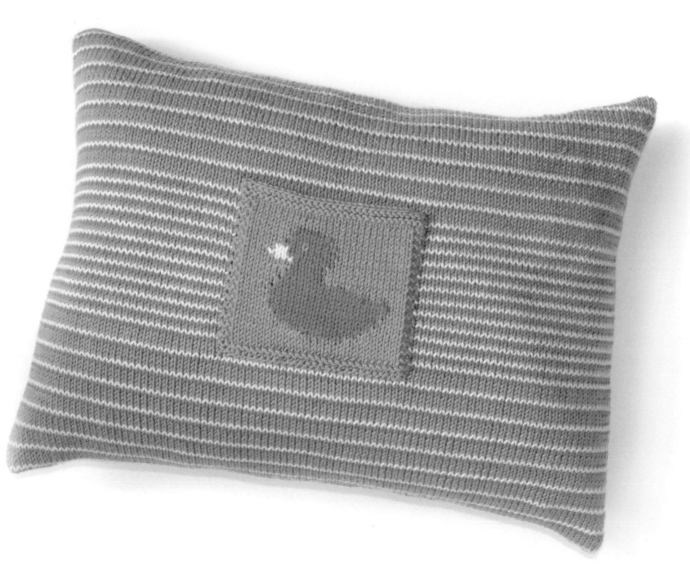

 Tip

Small pillows can often be washed complete with the pillow form. Check the care instructions of the pillow form when purchasing. This is handy if the project is to be used in a nursery.

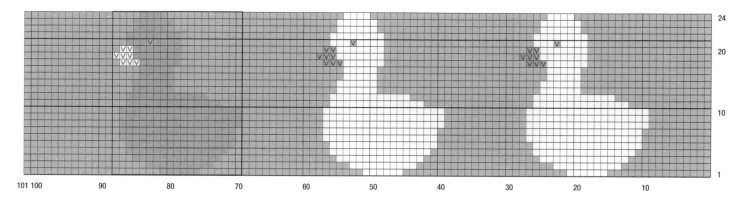

Back pocket

Using A, cast on 30 sts.

Knit 2 rows.

Row 3: Knit.

Row 4: K2, purl until last 2 sts, k2.

Repeat the last two rows once more.

For the following rows use the chart area outlined in red only.

Row 7: K5, work the first row of the chart, knit to the end of the row.

Row 8: K2, work the second row of the chart, purl until last 2 sts, k2.

Repeat the last two rows, working consecutive rows of the chart, until the chart has been completed.

Row 31: Knit.

Row 32: K2, purl until last 2 sts, k2.

Repeat the last two rows once more.

Knit two rows.

Bind off.

Finishing

Block lightly and duplicate stitch the eyes and beaks.

Weave in ends around the motifs.

Block the project to the measurements above.

Sew up side seams and weave in row ends into the seam stitches.

Insert pillow form. Remove filler or add filler depending on the form used. Using B, mattress stitch the top seam.

Tip

Straight needles provide more support to the stitches than circular needles. In intarsia knitting not all the stitches have the support of a neighboring stitch in the same yarn.

Cabled hottie

This is a classic and fabulously satisfying knit with an attractive cable pattern that is very easy to work.

Yarn
- Malabrigo Chunky, kettle-dyed 100% merino wool, 7 oz (100 g), 100 yd (91 m)
- 2 skeins

Measurements
- Cozy is designed to fit a standard hot water bottle of approximately 8½ x 13 in (22 x 33 cm)

Gauge
- Approximately 21 sts and 16 rows (unstretched) to 4 in (10 cm) over 1 x 1 rib using size 10 (6 mm) needles or size needed to obtain correct gauge
- Approximately 18 sts and 14 rows (unstretched) to 4 in (10 cm) over 1 x 1 rib using size 10½ (7 mm) needles or size needed to obtain correct gauge

Notions
- Size 10 (6 mm) and size 10½ (7 mm) 16-in (40-cm) long circular needles
- Stitch marker
- 6 small buttons (ensure these fit through the stitches of the knitting—on this size of needle, these should be large enough that buttonholes are not necessary)
- Cable needle
- Tapestry needle

Instructions

Cable panel
(NB Remember, this is worked in the round, so all cable rows are knit.)

Each cable worked over 12 sts.
Rows 1–5: k12.
Row 6: C6B, C6F.
Rep last 6 rows for pattern.

Using size 10½ (7 mm) needles, cast on 60 sts and join for working in the round, placing a marker for beg of round.
Rnd 1: p1, [k2, p2] twice, cable panel, [p2, k2] four times, p2, cable panel, [p2, k2] twice, p1.
Rep last rnd for pattern, until work measures approx 10 in (26 cm).
Next rnd: p1, [k2tog, p2tog] to last 3 sts, k3tog. 30 sts.
Next rnd: [p1, k1] to end of rnd.
Rep last rnd until rib measures approx 5½ in (14 cm).
Bind off all sts.

Weave in all ends.
Attach 6 small buttons evenly along bottom inside of cozy.
Slip cozy onto hot-water bottle, do up buttons along bottom, and fold down ribbed top.

Yarn alternatives
Any bulky yarn will do here; make sure you use a yarn with great stitch definition to let the cables shine.

Aran sweater tunic

A striking statement piece, this sweater is a perfect project for pushing your cabling skills.

Yarn
- Rooster Almerino DK, 50% baby alpaca/50% merino wool, 3½ oz (50 g), 124 yd (113 m)
- 15(15:17:18:19:20) balls

Measurements
- To fit bust

in	36	38	40	44
cm	92	96	102	112

Actual size

in	38	39½	41¾	45½
cm	96	100	106	116

Length

in	30¾	31	31½	32¼
cm	78	79	80	82

Sleeve seam

in	12	12	12½	12½
cm	30	30	32	32

Gauge
- 24 sts and 28 rows to 4 in (10 cm) over double seed st

Notions
- 1 pair each of size 4 (3.5 mm) and size 6 (4 mm) needles
- Stitch holders
- Tapestry needle

Instructions

Double seed st (across odd stitches)
Rnd 1 (RS): * k1, (p1, k1) to end of row.
Rnd 2: p1, (k1, p1) to end of row.
Rnd 3: p1, (k1, p1) to end of row.
Rnd 4: k1, (p1, k1) to end of row.
Rep these four rows for pattern.

Double seed st (across even stitches)
Row 1 (RS): (k1, p1) to end of row.
Row 2: (p1, k1) to end of row.
Row 3: (p1, k1) to end of row.
Row 4: (k1, p1) to end of row.
Rep these four rows for pattern.

Cable panel one
Each cable worked over 6 sts.
Row 1 (RS): k6.
Row 2: p6.
Rep last 2 rows once more.
Row 5: C6F.
Row 6: p6.
Rep last 6 rows for pattern.

Cable panel two
Each cable worked over 6 sts.
Row 1 (RS): k6.
Row 2: p6.
Rep last two rows once more.
Row 5: C6B.
Row 6: p6.
Rep last 6 rows for pattern.

Back

Using smaller needles, cast on 119(125:131:137:149:161) sts and work 1 in (3 cm) in 1 x 1 rib, ending with a WSR, then change to larger needles and work in double seed st until piece measures 7½ in (19 cm) from cast-on edge, ending with a WSR.

Shape for waist

Decrease 1 st at both ends of next and every foll 6th row until 113(119:125:131:143:155) sts, keeping double seed st pattern correct.

Now decrease 1 st at both ends of every foll 3rd row until 95(101:107:113:125:137) sts rem.

Work straight in double seed st without shaping until work measures 15½ in (39 cm) from cast-on edge.

Increase 1 st at both ends of next and every foll 6th row until 109(117:123:129:141:151) sts.

Now work straight on these sts until work measures 22(22¾:23¾:23¾:23:23¾) in/56(58:58:58:58.5:60) cm from cast-on edge.

Shape armholes

Bind off 5(5:6:6:8:9) sts at beg of next two rows, then dec 1 st at both ends of next and every foll row 0(0:0:3:5:7) times, then on every foll alt row until 83(87:89:91:95:97) sts rem.

Work straight in double seed st until armholes measure 7½(8:8½:8¾:9¼in:10) in/19(20:21:22:23.5:25) cm from armhole shaping, ending with a WSR.

Neck and shoulders

Next row (RS): bind off 7(8:8:8:8:8) sts, work 27(27:27:27:28:28) sts in pattern, place next 15(17:19:19:23:25) sts on holder for back neck, pattern across rem 34(35:35:35:36:36) sts.

Next row: bind off 7(8:8:8:8:8) sts, work to neck edge in pattern.

Next row: bind off 7 sts, pattern to end of row.

Next row: bind off 7(7:7:7:7:8) sts, work to last 2 sts, k2tog.

Next row: bind off 5(5:5:5:6:5) sts, work to end.
Bind off rem sts.
Rejoin yarn to right back neck and finish to match left back, reversing all shaping.

Front

Using smaller needles, cast on 119(125:131:137:149:161) sts and work 1 in (3 cm) in 1 x 1 rib, ending with a WSR and increasing 8 sts evenly across last row. 127(133:139:145:157:169) sts.

Change to larger needles and work for cables as follows:

Next row: double seed st pattern across 13(16:19:22:28:34) sts, (cable panel 1, double seed st across 13 sts) 3 times, (cable panei 2, double seed st across 13 sts) twice, cable panel 1, double seed st to end of row.

Work in cable pattern until piece measures 7½ in (19 cm) from cast-on edge, ending with a WSR.

Shape for waist.

Decrease 1 st at both ends of next and every foll 6th row until 121(127:133:139:151:163) sts, keeping cable/seed st pattern correct.

Now decrease 1 st at both ends of every foll 3rd row until 103(109:115:121:133:145) sts rem.

Work straight in double seed st without shaping until work measures 15½ in (39 cm) from cast-on edge.

Increase 1 st at both ends of next and every foll 6th row until 117(123:129:135:147:159) sts, bringing extra stitches into double seed st pattern.

Now work straight on these sts until work measures 22(22¾:23¾:23¾:23:23¾) in/56(58:58:58:58.5:60) cm from cast-on edge.

Shape armholes

Bind off 5(5:6:6:8:9) sts at beg of next two rows, then dec 1 st at both ends of next and every foll row 0(0:0:3:5:7) times, then on every foll alt row until 91(95:97:99:103:105) sts rem.

Work straight in double seed st and cable pattern until armholes measure 5½(6:6¼:6¼:7:7) in/14(15:16:16:18:18) cm from armhole shaping, ending with a WSR.

Neck and shoulders

Next row: pattern across 37(38:39:39:40:41) sts, bind off next 17(19:19:21:23:23) sts, decreasing 2 sts at center neck as you go, pattern to end of row.

Cont for right front as folls.

Work one row straight.

Next row (RS): bind off 5 sts, patt to end.

Bind off 4 sts at beg of foll alt row, 3 sts at beg of foll 1(1:2:2:33) alt rows and 2 sts at beg of foll 2(2:1:1:0:0) alt rows. 21(22:22:22:22:23) sts.

Cont straight until armhole matches back to shoulder, ending at armhole edge.

Next row (WS): bind off 7(8:8:8:8:8) sts, pattern across rem sts.

Now bind off 7 sts at beg of foll 2(2:2:2:2:1) alt rows, then bind off 8 sts at beg of foll 0(0:0:0:0:1) alt rows.

Rejoin yarn to left front neck and finish to match left back, reversing all shaping.

Sleeves

Using smaller needles, cast on 57(59:61:65:69:71) sts and work 1 in (3 cm) in 1 x 1 rib, ending with a WSR, then change to larger needles and work in double seed st, inc 1 st at both ends of 5th(3rd:5th:5th:5th:5th) row, then every foll 6th(6th:5th:5th:5th:5th) row, keeping double seed st correct, until there are 81(85:89:93:99:103) sts.

Work straight in double seed st until sleeve measures
12(12:12:12½:12½:13½) in/30(30:30:32:32:34) cm from cast-on edge,
ending with a WSR.

Shape cap

Bind off 5(5:6:6:7:8) sts at beg of next two rows, then dec 1 st at both
ends of next and every foll alt row until there are 49(51:53:57:61:61) sts,
then dec 1 st at both ends of every row until 21(21:21:23:25:29) sts
rem.

Bind off all sts.

Finishing

Block all pieces lightly, being careful not to flatten cables.

Join right shoulder seam.

Using smaller needles, pick up and knit 32(33:34:35:35:36) sts down left
front neck, pick up and knit 18(20:20:22:24:24) across front neck, pick
up and knit 32(33:34:34:34:35) sts up right front neck, pick up and knit
13 sts from back right neck, knit 15(17:19:19:23:25) sts from back
holder, pick up and knit 13sts from back left neck.
123(127:131:137:143:147) sts.

Work 4 rows in 1 x 1 rib on these sts, then cast off very loosely in rib.

Join rem shoulder and collar seam.

Set in sleeves.

Sew up underarm and side seams neatly.

Weave in all ends.

Yarn alternatives

Any DK weight yarn with a good stitch definition will work
well here.

Lacy socks

This is a pretty alternative to the simple sock pattern—these socks are fun and satisfying to knit and a pleasure to wear.

Yarn
- Juno Fibre Arts Alice Sock Hand Dyed Yarn, 70% baby alpaca/20% silk/10% cashmere, 7 oz (100 g), 440 yd (400 m)

Measurements
- To fit S(M:L) adult female feet. It is easy to adjust the length of the foot or the height of the sock up the leg by knitting more or fewer rows where indicated

Gauge
- 32 sts and 40 rows to 4 in (10 cm) over St st using size 2 (2.75 mm) needles or size needed to obtain correct gauge

Notions
- 1 set each of 2.5 mm and size 2 (2.75 mm) double-pointed needles.

Yarn alternatives
Any sock yarn will substitute here.

Instructions

Diamond lace pattern
Rnd 1 (RS): *k1, k2tog, yo, k1, yo, ktog tbl; rep from * to last st, k1.
Rnd 2 (and every other rnd): knit.
Rnd 3: k2tog, *yo, k3, yo, sl next two sts, k1, p2sso; rep from * to last 5 sts, yo, k3, yo, k2tog tbl.
Rnd 5: *k1, yo, k2tog tbl, k1, k2tog, yo; rep from * to last st, k1.
Rnd 7: k2, *yo, sl next two sts, k1, p2sso, yo, k3; rep from * to last 5 sts, yo, sl next two sts, k1, p2sso, yo, k2.
Row 8: knit.
Rep last 8 rows.

Using smaller needles, cast on 60(66:72) sts and spread over dpns for working in the rnd.
Work 10 rnds 1 x 1 rib, increasing one st at end of last row. 61(67:73) sts.

Change to larger needles and begin to work in lace pattern until work is approx 6 in (15 cm) from cast-on edge or desired length of leg.

Shape heel
Work across first 31(37:37) sts in pattern and leave on needle for working instep later.

K rem 30(36:36) sts for heel and begin to work backward and forward on these sts as folls:
Next row (WS): Sl 1, [p1, sl 1] to end.
Next row [RS]: K all sts.
Repeat last 2 rows 23(24:25) times more.

Turn heel
Row 1 [RS]: k17(19:19), ssk, k1, turn work.
Row 2: Sl 1, p5(3:3), p2tog, p1, turn work.
Row 3: Sl 1, k6(4:4), ssk, k1, turn work.

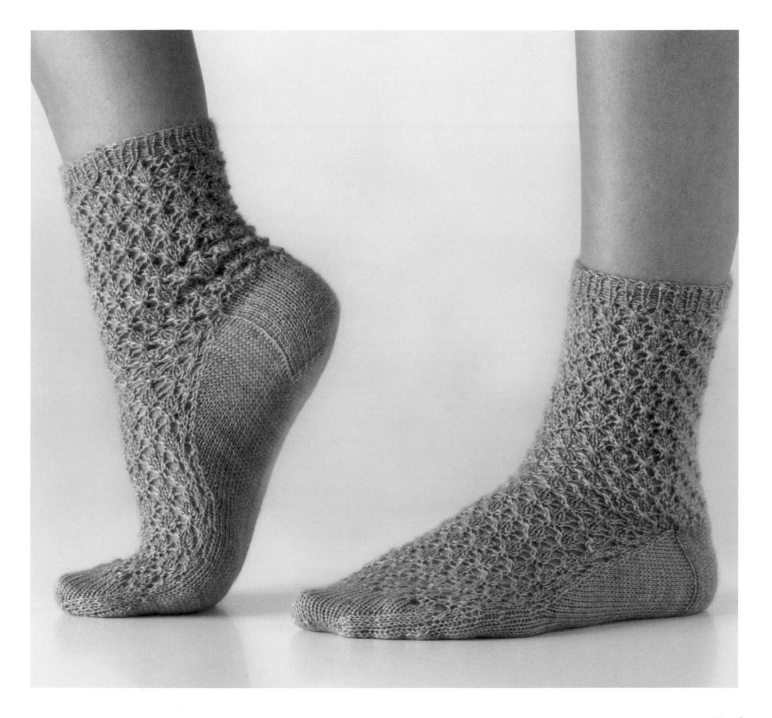

Row 4: Sl 1, p7(5:5), p2tog, p1, turn work.
Row 5: Sl 1, k8(6:6), ssk, k1, turn work.
Row 6: Sl 1, p9(7:7) p2tog, p1, turn work.
Row 7: Sl 1, k10(8:8) ssk, k1, turn work.
Row 8: Sl 1, p11(9:9) p2tog, p1, turn work.
Row 9: Sl 1, k12(10:10) ssk, k1, turn work.
Row 10: Sl 1, p13(11:11) p2tog, p1, turn work.
Row 11: Sl 1, k14(12:12), ssk, k1, turn work.
Row 12: Sl 1, p15(13:13) p2tog, p1, turn work.

Small size only
18 sts. Proceed to gusset.

Medium and large sizes
Row 13: Sl 1, k14, ssk, k1, turn work.
Row 14: Sl 1, p15 p2tog, p1, turn work.
Row 15: Sl 1, k16, ssk, k1, turn work.
Row 16: Sl 1, p17 p2tog, p1, turn work.
20 sts. Proceed to gusset.

Gusset
k9(10) sts, change to 2nd needle, k9(10) sts, continuing with this needle, pick up and k 24(25:26) sts (use each slipped st as a guide) along edge of heel flap. 33(35:36) sts.

Using 2nd needle, pattern across instep sts. 31(37:37) sts.

Using 3rd needle, pick up and k 24(25:26) sts along edge of heel flap as other side of heel, k first 9(10) sts of heel flap. 33(35:36) sts.

Cont on these 97(107:109) sts in the round.
Next round: k to last 2 sts on 1st needle, k2tog, patt across instep sts, ssk, k to end of rnd. 2 sts decreased.
Next round: k all sts on 1st needle, patt across instep sts, k to end of rnd.
Rep these two rnds until there are 57(61:67) sts.

Instep

Cont in patt, working sts on needle 1 and needle 3 in stockinette st and sts on needle 2 in patt as set, until foot measures approx 1½ in (4 cm) less than desired length, ending with a rnd 3 or rnd 7 of lace pattern.

Work one rnd straight, redistributing sts over needles and decreasing 1 st so that there are 14(15:16) sts on 1st needle, 28(30:33) on second needle, and 14(15:17) on 3rd needle. 56(60:66) sts.

Next round: knit.

Next round: k to last 3 sts on 1st needle, k2tog, k1, k1, ssk, k to last 3 sts on 2nd needle, k2tog, k1, k1, ssk, k to end of rnd. 4 sts decreased. Repeat last 2 rounds until 24(26:28) sts rem.

Place sts evenly on two needles, break yarn, leaving enough to work seam, then graft together toe.

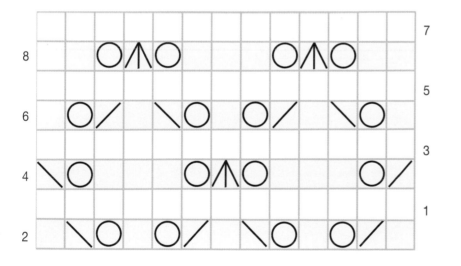

Fair Isle yoke sweater

This sweater is worked in the round, from the bottom upward for minimal finishing, which makes for a speedy and fun knit.

Yarn

- Debbie Bliss Baby Cashmerino, 55% merino wool/33% microfiber/12% cashmere, 3½ oz (50 g), 136 yd (125 m)
- 4(5:5:6:7) balls of yarn A: shade 009, Gray
- 1 ball each: Yarn B: shade 601, Pink; Yarn C: shade 018, Green; Yarn D: shade 50, Coral

Measurements

CHILD	S	M	L
To fit chest			
in	24	25¾	27
cm	60	65	70
Actual size			
in	25¾	27	29½
cm	65	70	75
Length			
in	14¼	16	17
cm	36	40	43
Sleeve seam			
in	10	11	12½
cm	26	28	31

Gauge

- 24 sts and 36 sts to 4 in (10 cm) over St st using size 5 (3.75 mm) needles or size needed to obtain correct gauge.

Notions

- 1 pair each of size 5 (3.75 mm) and size 3 (3.25 mm) 24–in (60–cm) circular needles
- 1 set each of size 5 (3.75 mm) and size 3 (3.25 mm) double-pointed needles
- Stitch marker
- Tapestry needle

Instructions

Body and arms worked from bottom up separately, then joined at yoke.

Body

Using smaller circular needles, cast on 156(168:180) sts and join for working in the round, being careful not to twist stitches and placing marker at beg of round, work 8 rows 1 x 1 rib.

Change to larger needles and work in St st for 8½(9:10) in/21(23:25) cm or desired length to underarm, ending last rnd 4 sts before end of rnd. Bind off for armholes as folls:

Next rnd: bind off next 8 sts, k 70(76:82) sts, bind off 8 sts, work to end of rnd.

Sleeves

Using smaller double pointed needles, cast on 36(42:42) sts and join for working in the round, being careful not to twist stitches and placing marker at beg of round, work 8 rows 1 x 1 rib.

Change to larger needles and work in st st, increasing 1 st at both ends of round every 7th(8th:8th) rnd until 58(64:66) sts.

Cont straight if necessary until sleeve measures 10(11:12½) in/26(28:31) cm or desired length to underarm, ending last rnd 4 sts before end of rnd.

Bind off 8 sts and then work to end of rnd. 50(56:58) sts.

Yoke

With RSF, knit across 50(56:58) sts of sleeve, then 70(76:82) sts of front, then 50(56:58) sts of rem sleeve and finally 70(76:82) sts of back. 240(264:280) sts.

Pm for beg of rnd and cont in the rnd on these sts.

Change to yarn B and work one rnd, change to yarn C and work 1 rnd, now work 12 rows of Fair Isle chart all round yoke, using yarn D for contrast color.

Measurements

BABY SIZE:

	XS	S	M	L
To fit chest				
in	18	22	24	26
cm	46	56	61	66
Actual size				
in	20	24	26	28
cm	51	61	66	71
Length				
in	12	13	14	16
cm	30	33	35	40
Sleeve seam				
in	8	11½	12¼	13
cm	21	29	31	33

ADULT FEMALE

	S	M	L
To fit chest			
in	33	35	37
cm	84	89	94
Actual size			
in	35	37	39
cm	89	94	99
Length			
in	21½	22½	23½
cm	55	57	60
Sleeve seam			
in	19	19¾	21
cm	48	50	54

ADULT MALE

	S	M	L
To fit chest			
in	39	42	46
cm	99	107	117
Actual size			
in	41	44	48
cm	104	112	122
Length			
in	25½	26½	27
cm	65	67	69
Sleeve seam			
in	22	23	23½
cm	56	58	60

After 12 rnds, work 1 rnd in yarn C and then 1 rnd yarn B. Change to yarn A and work one rnd, then dec as folls:

Next rnd: (k3, k2tog) to last 0(4:0) sts, k0(4:0). 192(212:224) sts. Work 3 further rnds in yarn A, then work 1 rnd yarn B. change to yarn C and work straight until work measures 3¼(3½:4) in/8(9:10) cm, then work 1 rnd in yarn B, then 1 rnd in yarn A.

Next rnd: (k2, k2tog) to end of rnd. 144(159:168) sts.

Work 3 further rnds in yarn A.

Now work 1 rnd in yarn B, then one rnd in yarn C, then cont straight in yarn C until work measures approx 4½(5:5½) in/11(12:14) cm, then work 1 rnd in yarn B, then 1 rnd in yarn A.

Next rnd: (k1, k2tog) to end of rnd. 96(106:112) sts. Cont in yarn A until yoke measures approx 5¾(6½:7) in/14.5(16.5:17.5) cm.

Shape back neck with short rows as folls:
Knit to left shoulder center, turn, leaving rem sts unworked and work across to right shoulder center, turn, leaving rem sts unworked and work back to 7 sts before left shoulder turn, turn and work back to 7 sts before right shoulder turn, turn and work 1 rnd, working over all sts.

Next rnd: (k1, k2tog) to last 0(1:1) st, k(1:1). 64(71:75) sts.

Neckband

Work in 1 x 1 rib, increasing 1 st on first row of M and L sizes, for 4 rows, bind off all sts loosely in rib.

Block lightly to shape, paying particular attention to the Fair Isle band, which will pull in slightly, and then sew up underarm seams and weave in all ends.

Yarn alternatives
Any sportweight yarns will substitute here.

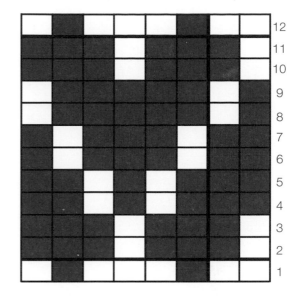

Advanced Projects

Lace panel gloves

This is a simple first glove pattern, with a pretty lace pattern for an easy embellishment.

Yarn

- Madeline Tosh Pashmina, 75% superwash wool/15% silk/10% cashmere, 7 oz (100 g), 360 yd (328 m)
- 1 ball of shade windowpane

Measurements

- To fit average adult female hand.

Gauge

- Approximately 26 sts and 34 rows to 4in (10 cm) using size 4 (3.5 mm) needles

Notions

- 1 set each of size 4 (3.5 mm) and size 3 (3.25 mm) double-pointed needles
- Stitch holders

Yarn alternatives

Any 4ply sockweight yarn will substitute here; try to choose one that is spun tightly or includes some manmade fiber to ensure that the gloves are durable.

Instructions

Lace panel (worked over 7 sts)
Row 1 (RS): p2, (k5, p2) to end of row.
Row 2: k2, (p5, k2) to end of row.
Row 3: p2, * k2tog, yo, k1, yo, sl1, k1, psso, p2; rep from * to end of row.
Row 4: rep row 2.
Rep last 4 rows for pattern.

Using size 3 (3.25 mm) dpns, cast on 42 sts and spread work evenly over 3 dpns for working in the round.
Work 2¾ in (7 cm) in 1 x 1 rib.
On last round, increase 7 sts evenly. 49 sts.
Change to larger needles.
Next rnd: k34, work lace panel over next 7 sts, k to end of rnd.
Work 3 further rnds as last.

Place thumb gusset

Rnd 5: k1, inc into each of next 2 sts, k to lace panel, work panel, k to end. 51 sts.
Rnd 6: k to lace panel, work lace panel over next 7 sts, k to end of rnd.
Rep last rnd once more.
Rnd 8: k1, inc in next st, k2, inc in next st, k to lace panel, work panel, k to end of rnd. 53 sts.
Rnds 9 and 10: rep rnd 6.
Rnd 11: k1, inc in next st, k4, inc in next st, k to lace panel, work panel, k to end of rnd. 55 sts.
Rnds 12 and 13: rep rnd 6.
Rnd 14: k1, inc in next st, k6, inc in next st, k to lace panel, work panel, k to end of rnd. 57 sts.
Rnds 15 and 16: rep rnd 6.
Rnd 17: k1, inc in next st, k8, inc in next st, k to lace panel, work panel, k to end of rnd. 59 sts.

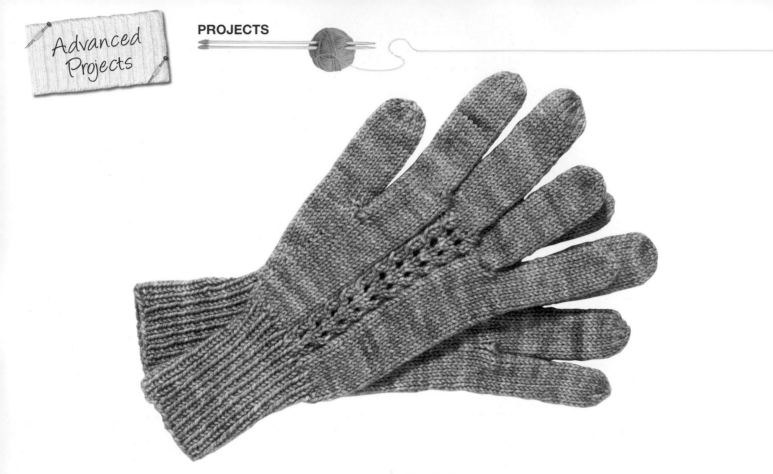

Rnds 18 and 19: rep rnd 6.

Rnd 20: k1, inc in next st, k10, inc in next st, k to lace panel, work panel, k to end of rnd. 61 sts.

Work 7 rnds straight in pattern without shaping.

Next rnd: k1, slip next 14 sts onto a holder for thumb, cast on 4 sts and pattern to end. 51 sts.

Work 12 rows straight on these sts.

Split for fingers—each finger worked in the rnd.

Index finger

k8, slip all of next sts but final 6 onto holders/waste yarn, cast on 2 sts, k6 (last sts). 16 sts.

Work 28 rnds straight on these sts.

Shape top of finger.

Next rnd: (k2tog) across rnd. 8 sts.

Work 1 rnd straight on these 8 sts, then break yarn, thread through rem sts, pull up to close finger, and secure.

Middle finger

Rejoin yarn and k next 6 sts from holder, cast on 2 sts, k last 7 sts of round from holder, pick up 2 sts from base of index finger. 17 sts.

Work 34 rnds straight on these sts.

Shape top of finger.

Next rnd: (k2tog) to last st, k1. 9 sts.

Work 1 rnd straight on these 9 sts, then break yarn, thread through rem sts, pull up to close finger, and secure.

Ring finger

Rejoin yarn and k next 6 sts from holder, cast on 2 sts, k last 6 sts of round from holder, pick up 2 sts from base of middle finger. 16 sts.

Complete as index finger.

Little finger

Rejoin yarn and k rem 12 sts from holder, pick up 2 sts from base of ring finger. 14 sts.

Work 24 rnds straight on these sts.

Shape top of finger

Next rnd: (k2tog) to end. 7 sts.

Work 1 rnd straight on these 7 sts, then break yarn, thread through rem sts, pull up to close finger, and secure.

Thumb

Rejoin yarn to thumb sts, k14 from holder, pick up 4 sts from cast-on sts. 18 sts.

Work 23 rnds straight in the rnd.

Shape top

Next rnd: (k2tog) to end. 9 sts.

Work 1 rnd straight on these 9 sts, then break yarn, thread through rem sts, pull up to close finger, and secure.

Left glove

Using size 3 (3.25 mm) dpns, cast on 42 sts and spread work evenly over 3 dpns for working in the round.

Work 2¾ in (7 cm) in 1 x 1 rib.

On last round, increase 7 sts evenly. 49 sts.

Change to larger needles.

Next rnd: k8, work lace panel over next 7 sts, k to end of rnd.

Work 3 further rnds as last.

Place thumb gusset

Rnd 5: work in pattern as established to last 3 sts, inc into each of next 2 sts, k1. 51 sts.

Rnd 6: k to lace panel, work lace panel over next 7 sts, k to end of rnd. Rep last rnd once more.

Rnd 8: work in pattern as established to last 5 sts, inc in next st, k2, inc in next st, k1. 53 sts.

Rnds 9 and 10: rep rnd 6.

Rnd 11: work in pattern as established to last 7 sts, inc in next st, k4, inc in next st, k1. 55 sts.

Rnds 12 and 13: rep rnd 6.

Rnd 14: work in pattern as established to last 9 sts, inc in next st, k6, inc in next st, k to lace panel, work panel, k to end of rnd. 57 sts.

Rnds 15 and 16: rep rnd 6.

Rnd 17: work in pattern as established to last 11 sts, inc in next st, k8, inc in next st, k to lace panel, work panel, k to end of rnd. 59 sts.

Rnds 18 and 19: rep rnd 6.

Rnd 20: work in pattern as established to last 13 sts, inc in next st, k10, inc in next st, k to lace panel, work panel, k to end of rnd. 61 sts.

Work 7 rnds straight in pattern without shaping.

Next rnd: work in pattern as established to last 15 sts, cast on 4 sts, slip next 14 sts onto a holder for thumb, k1. 51 sts.

Work 12 rows straight on these sts.

Split for fingers—each finger worked in the rnd.

Index finger

k6, slip all of next sts but final 8 onto holders/waste yarn, cast on 2 sts, k8 (last sts). 16 sts.

Work 28 rnds straight on these sts.

Shape top of finger as for right hand's index finger.

Middle finger

Rejoin yarn and k next 7 sts from holder, cast on 2 sts, k last 6 sts of round from holder, pick up 2 sts from base of index finger. 17 sts.

Work 34 rnds straight on these sts.

Shape top of finger as right hand's middle finger.

Ring finger: rejoin yarn and k next 6 sts from holder, cast on 2 sts, k last 6 sts of round from holder, pick up 2 sts from base of middle finger. 16 sts.

Shape top of finger as right hand's ring finger.

Little finger

Rejoin yarn and k rem 12 sts from holder, pick up 2 sts from base of ring finger. 14 sts.

Work 24 rnds straight on these sts.

Shape top of finger as right hand's little finger.

Thumb

Work as for right-hand thumb.

Finishing

Weave in all ends and block lightly.

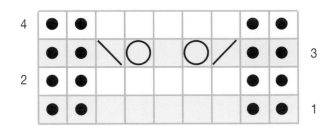

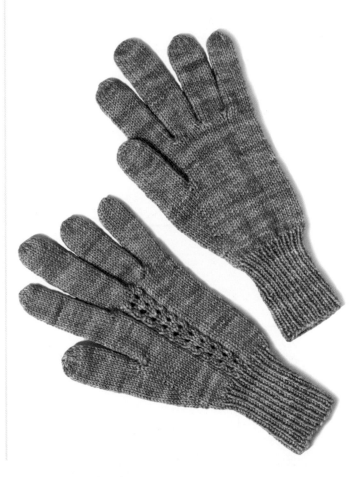

Fair Isle cardigan coat

There's a lot of Fair Isle in this pattern, but very little shaping, so it's a perfect project for a nervous knitter.

Yarn

- Jamieson and Smith Shetland Supreme Jumper Weight, 100% Shetland wool, 3½ oz (50 g), 188 yd (177 m)
- 3(3:4:5) balls of yarn A: shade 2003, Shaela
- 2(2:3:3) balls of yarn B: shade 2004, Moorit
- 2(2:3:3) balls of yarn C: shade 2009, Yuglet
- 1(1:2:2) balls of yarn D: shade 2007, Sholmit
- 1(1:2:2) balls of yarn E: shade 2002, Mooskit
- 1(1:2:2) balls of yarn F: shade 2006, Gaulmogot
- 1(1:2:2) balls of yarn G: shade 2001, White

Measurements

To fit bust

in	32–34	36–38	40–42	44–46
cm	81–86	91–97	102–107	112–117

Length

in	16	17¾	19¾	21½
cm	40	45	50	55

Sleeve seam

in	20½	21¼	22	22½
cm	52	54	56	57

Gauge

- 32 sts and 40 rows to 4 in (10 cm) over St st using size 2 (2.75 mm) needles or size needed to obtain correct gauge.

Notions

- 1 set each of 2.5 mm and size 2 (2.75 mm) double-pointed needles.

Instructions

For Fair Isle pattern, follow chart from row 1 (see page 173).
For the colored pattern squares, alternate stripes of yarn B and yarn C, changing color after every whole pattern repeat of 62 rows.
For background, or blank pattern squares, alternate stripes of rem yarns as folls:

Stripe sequence (12 rows of each color)

Yarn D.
Yarn A.
Yarn E.
Yarn F.
Yarn G.
Yarn F.
Yarn E.
Yarn A.

Sleeves

Using smaller needles and yarn A, cast on 59(63:67:71) sts and work in 1 x 1 rib for 6 in (15 cm).
Change to larger needles and work straight in St st beg with a k row, increasing 1 st at both ends of 15th(17th:17th:15th) row and every following 16th(17th:18th:16th) row until 73(77:81:87) sts.
Work straight until work measures 20½(21¼:22:22½) in/52(54:56:57) cm from cast-on edge or desired length to underarm.
Bind off 5 sts at beg of next 2 rows, then work straight for 2½(2¾:3:3) in/6(7:8:8) cm.
Bind off all sts.

Body

Cast on 138(150:162:174) sts and work straight in Fair Isle pattern as set by chart and stripe sequence until work measures 16(17¾:19¾:21½ in/40(45:50:55) cm from cast-on edge, ending with a WSR.

Fair Isle chart

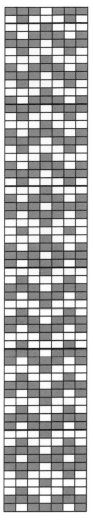

Left armhole

Next row (RS): pattern across 56(62:69:77) sts, bind off 43(46:50:52) sts, pattern to end.

Work 5 rows straight on these 39(42:43:45) sts, leaving rem sts on holder, for 5 rows.

Break yarn, leave sts on holder, and rejoin yarn to unworked sts with WSF and work 5 rows on these 56(62:69:77) sts.

Cast on 43(46:50:52) sts over the armhole, pick up sts on holder, and work across.

Next row: work across all sts.**

Cont straight in Fair Isle pattern until work measures 17(19:21:23) in/ 43(48.5:53.5:58.5) cm from left armhole.

Right armhole

Rep between ** and **.

Work straight in Fair Isle pattern until work measures 16(17¾:19¾:21½ in/ 40(45:50:55) cm from right armhole.

Bind off all sts.

Finishing

Set in sleeves to armholes and sew up underarm seam.

Yarn alternatives

Any sportweight yarn will substitute here; try to choose a wool-rich yarn for the "stickiness" needed to create neat Fair Isle.

Lace stole

If you have mastered the basic lace scarf (see page 136) and want to try something a little more challenging, try your hand at this pretty stole.

Yarn
- Malabrigo Lace, 100% baby merino wool, 3½ oz (50 g), 470 yd (430 m)
- 2 skeins of shade 30, Purple Mystery

Measurements
- 16.5 x 45 in (42 x 115 cm)

Gauge
- 29 st and 36 rows to 4 in (10 cm) over lace pattern

Notions
- 1 pair of size 7 (4.5 mm) needles
- Tapestry needle

Instructions

Lace pattern 1 (multiple of 12 sts, plus 3)
Row 1: k1, k2tog, k4, yo, k1, yo, k4, *sl1, k2tog, psso, k4, yo, k1, yo, k4; rep from * to last 3 sts, sl 1, k1 psso, k1.
Row 2: purl.
Rep last 2 rows 3 more times.
Row 9: k2, yo, k4, sl1, k2tog, psso, k4, yo, *k1, yo, k4, sl1, k2tog, psso, k4, yo; rep from * to last 2 sts, k2.
Row 10: purl.
Rep last 2 rows 3 more times.
These 16 rows form pattern.

Lace pattern 2 (multiple of 12 sts, plus 3)
Row 1: k1, k2tog, k4, yo, k1, yo, k4, *sl1, k2tog, psso, k4, yo, k1, yo, k4; rep from * to last 3 sts, sl 1, k1 psso, k1.
Row 2: purl.
Row 3: k1, k2tog, k2, yo, k5, yo, k2, *sl1, k2tog, psso, k2, yo, k5, yo, k2; rep from * to last 3 sts, sl 1, k1 psso, k1.
Row 4: purl.
Rep rows 1 and 2 twice more.
Row 9: k2, yo, k4, sl1, k2tog, psso, k4, yo, *k1, yo, k4, sl1, k2tog, psso, k4, yo; rep from * to last 2 sts, k2.
Row 10: purl.
Row 11: k4, yo, k2, sl1, k2tog, psso, k2, yo, *k5, yo, k2, sl1, k2tog, psso, k2, yo; rep from * to last 4 sts, k4.
Row 12: purl.
Rep rows 9 and 10 twice more.
These 16 rows form pattern.

Yarn alternatives
Any laceweight yarn will achieve the same effect. However you can try other weights of yarn and change the needle size accordingly.

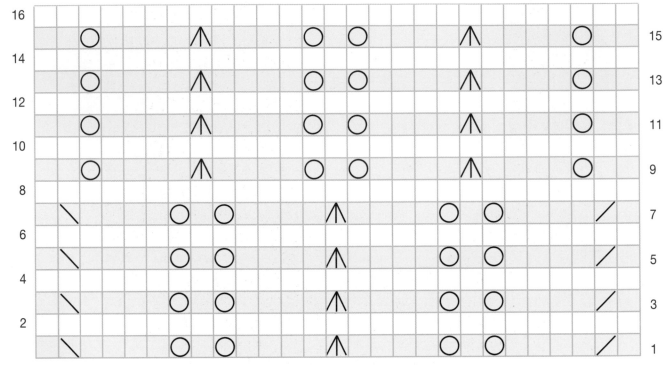

Lace pattern 1

Using size 7 (4.5 mm) needles, cast on 123 sts and work in St st for 4 rows, beg with a k row.

Beg lace pattern 1 and work 3 repeats.

Change to lace pattern 2 and work for approx 52 in (130 cm) or desired length minus 8 in (20 cm), ending with last row of pattern.

Change back to lace pattern 1 and work 3 repeats.

Bind off all sts.

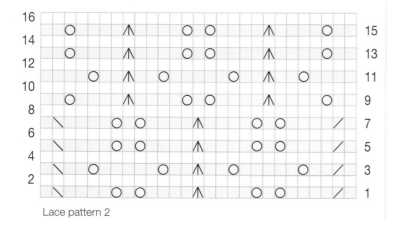

Lace pattern 2

Cabled afghan

This project makes an incredibly warm and stylish blanket for wintry weather.

Yarn
- Brown Sheep Burly Spun, 100% wool, 8 oz (226 g), 132 yd (121 m)
- 2 balls each of
  Yarn A: shade BS10, Cream
  Yarn B: shade BS115, Oatmeal
  Yarn C: shade BS08, Wild Oak
  Yarn D: shade BS03, Gray Heather

Measurements
- Approx 49 in wide (124 cm) and 60 in (150 cm) length

Gauge
- 10 sts and 14 rows to 4 in (10 cm) over St st using size 15 (10 mm) needles or size required to obtain correct gauge.

Notions
- Pair of size 15 (10 mm) needles
- Cable needle
- Tapestry needle

Yarn alternatives
Any bulky yarn will substitute here; choosing different weights will simply cause your blanket to become smaller or larger.

Instructions

You may wish to use a long circular needle for this pattern, but continue knitting straight; this way the weight of the bulky yarn will fall onto your lap on the cord, which will be more comfortable to work with (as opposed to at the end of unwieldy long needles).

Beg each panel from row 1 on row 1 of main pattern, where indicated.

Panel 1
Z-twist cable panel.
Each cable worked over 6 sts.
Row 1 (RS): k6.
Row 2: p6.
Rep last 2 rows once more.
Row 5: C6B.
Row 6: p6.
Rep last 6 rows for pattern.

Panel 2
Braided cable panel.
Cable worked over 9 sts.
Row 1 (RS): knit.
Row 2: purl.
Row 3: k3, C6F.
Row 4: purl.
Row 5: knit.
Row 6: purl.
Row 7: C6B, k2.
Row 8: purl.
Rep last 8 rows for pattern.

Panel 3

S-twist cable panel.

Each cable worked over 6 sts.

Row 1 (RS): k6.

Row 2: p6.

Rep last 2 rows once more.

Row 5: C6F.

Row 6: p6.

Rep last 6 rows for pattern.

Main Pattern

Using size 15 (10 mm) needles, and Yarn A, cast on 123 sts.

Row 1: (k15, cable panel 1) twice, k15, cable panel 2, (k15, cable panel 3) twice, k15.

Row 2: (k5, p5, k5, cable panel 3) twice, k5, p5, k5, cable panel 2, (k5, p5, k5, cable panel 1) twice, k5, p5, k5.

Rep last 2 rows for pattern.

Cont in pattern, working 4–in (10–cm) stripes of each color until blanket measures approx 59 in (150 cm), ending with a row 2.

Stitch directory

The following pages showcase over 100 different stitches to practice, building up from easy, to intermediate, then advanced and lace and cables. Trying a swatch of each is the perfect way to build upon your techniques and knowledge, and if you turn the resulting swatches into the patchwork blanket on page 96, you will not even waste any yarn.

Easy

The first set of stitches showcases simply the basics—working with the knit stitch and the purl stitch. As you try the swatches, it will become clear how many pretty textures you can create with just the most basic of stitches.

Garter stitch

The simplest of knit fabrics, garter stitch is reversible—being the same on both sides. This means it doesn't curl, and therefore is great for adding edgings to areas of stockinette. Each "ridge" counts as two rows, so you usually get far more rows per 4 in (10 cm) than by using the same yarn in stockinette stitch.

Cast on any number of sts and knit every row.

Stockinette stitch

Stockinette is the most commonly used stitch in knitting, especially in mass-produced knitwear. It produces a smooth and familiar fabric, which curls at the edges, because different stitches are knitted on each side of the fabric—knit on the right side and purl on the wrong side.

Cast on any number of sts.

Row 1 (RS): knit.

Row 2 (WS): purl.

Rep last 2 rows for pattern.

Reverse stockinette stitch

This fabric is the name for the back of stockinette stitch—it is the purl, or wrong, side of stockinette stitch used as the right side, so you purl all right-side rows and knit all wrong-side rows.

Cast on any number of sts.

Row 1 (RS): purl.

Row 2 (WS): knit.

Rep last 2 rows for pattern.

Twisted stockinette stitch

Stockinette stitch, but working all knit rows through the back of the stitch.

Cast on any number of sts.

Row 1 (RS): knit into back (tbl) of every stitch.

Row 2 (WS): purl.

Rep last 2 rows for pattern.

Welting

A welted fabric is the name for one composed of horizontal "ribs," a mixture of stockinette and reverse stockinette stitch in stripes. The smallest number of repeats you can work to create welts is four rows.

Cast on any number of sts.

Row 1 (RS): knit.

Row 2: purl.

Row 3: purl.

Row 4: knit.

Rep last 4 rows for pattern.

1 x 1 rib

The most basic of ribs, alternating knit and purl stitches across the row. It can be worked over any number of stitches, but is usually worked over an odd number. It is reversible and very stretchy; great for cuffs.

Cast on an odd number of sts.

Row 1 (RS): k1, (p1, k1) to end of row.

Row 2: p1, (k1, p1) to end of row.

Rep last 2 rows for pattern.

Or

Cast on an even number of sts.

Row 1 (RS): (k1, p1) to end of row.

Rep last row for pattern.

Woven rib

Once you can knit and purl and know how to change between the two across a row, you can play with a variation of all of the basic stitches. This stitch is a mixture of 1 x 1 rib and garter stitch.

Cast on an odd number of sts.

Row 1 (RS): knit.

Row 2: knit.

Row 3: p1, (k1, p1) to end of row.

Row 4: k1, (p1, k1) to end of row.

Rep last 2 rows for pattern.

2 x 3 rib

Just because the 1 x 1 and 2 x 2 ribs are most common, does not mean you have to use the same numbers of knits and purls across the row—there are multiple variations you can play with.

Cast on a multiple of 5 sts, plus 3.

Row 1 (RS): k3, (p2, k3) to end of row.

Row 2: p3, (k2, p3) to end of row.

Rep last 2 rows for pattern.

Twisted rib

This is a variation on 1 x 1 rib and twisted stockinette stitch, creating a rib that has more definition.

Cast on an odd number of sts.

Row 1 (RS): p1, (k1tbl, p1) to end of row.

Row 2: k1, (p1tbl, k1) to end of row.

Rep last 2 rows for pattern.

2 x 2 rib

This is a variation of 1 x 1 rib, but, unlike the 1 x 1, you can more easily see the recessed purl stitches, making it a common choice for edgings.

Cast on a multiple of 4 sts, plus 2.

Row 1 (RS): k2, (p2, k2) to end of row.

Row 2: p2, (k2, p2) to end of row.

Rep last 2 rows for pattern.

Broken 1 x 1 rib

A mixture of 1 x 1 rib and purl.

Cast on an odd number of sts.

Row 1 (RS): k1, (p1, k1) to end of row.

Row 2: purl.

Rep last 2 rows for pattern.

Broken 2 x 2 rib

This is a mixture of 2 x 2 rib and purl.

Cast on a multiple of 4 sts, plus 2.

Row 1 (RS): k2, (p2, k2) to end of row.

Row 2: purl to end of row.

Rep last 2 rows for pattern.

Intermediate

When you know how to make knits and purls and can change between the two across a row to make ribs, you can begin playing with them to make textures.

Seed stitch

A seed (or moss) stitch is basically a 1 x 1 rib, but instead of stacking all the stitches into vertical ribs, with the purl stitches recessed, the knits and purls turn into diagonal lines, with the purls more pronounced as little dots. A very pretty stitch and, as it is reversible, very stable and fabulous for edgings. Like 1 x 1 rib, it can be worked over any number of stitches, but is usually worked over an odd number.

Cast on an odd number of sts.
Row 1 (RS): k1 (p1, p1) to end of row.
Rep this row for pattern.
Or
Cast on an even number of sts.
Row 1 (RS): (k1, p1) to end of row.
Row 2: (p1, k1) to end of row.
Rep last 2 rows for pattern.

Seed stitch ribs

This is an attractive mixture of seed stitch and rib.
Cast on a multiple of 8 sts, plus 3.
Row 1: k3, *(p1, k1) twice, p1, k3; rep from * to end of row.
Row 2: p3, *k2, p1, k2, p3; rep from * to end of row.
Rep last 2 rows for pattern.

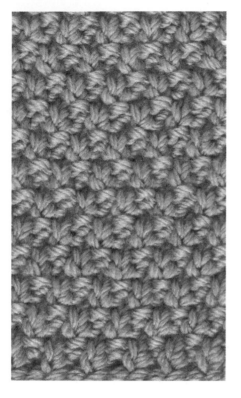

Double seed stitch

This is a version of seed stitch worked over four rows.

Cast on an odd number of sts.

Row 1 (RS): k1, (p1, k1) to end of row.

Row 2: p1, (k1, p1) to end of row.

Row 3: p1, (k1, p1) to end of row.

Row 4: k1, (p1, k1) to end of row.

Rep last 4 rows for pattern.

Broken welt stitch

This uses a similar theme as seed stitch for the knitted welts.

Cast on a multiple of 10 sts.

Rows 1–4: (k5, p5) to end of row.

Row 5: knit.

Rows 6–9: (p5, k5) to end of row.

Row 10: purl.

Rep last 10 rows for pattern.

Dot stitch

This is a very pretty use of the purl stitch within a stockinette stitch fabric; you can adapt this to create whatever pattern you wish with the purls.

Cast on a multiple of 4 sts plus 3.

Row 1 (RS): k1 (p1, k3) to last 2sts, p1, k1.

Row 2: purl.

Row 3: (k3, p1) to last 3 sts, k3.

Row 4: purl.

Rep last 4 rows for pattern.

Small blocks

A variation on double seed stitch, but using pairs of stitches.

Cast on a multiple of 4 sts, plus 2.

Row 1 (RS): k2 (p2, k2) to end of row.

Row 2: p2, (k2, p2) to end of row.

Row 3: p2, (k2, p2) to end of row.

Row 4: k2 (p2, k2) to end of row.

Rep last 4 rows for pattern.

Basket weave

The same theme as small blocks, but with differing multiples for a more defined check.

Cast on a multiple of 6 sts, plus 3.

Row 1 (RS): k3 (p3, k3) to end of row.

Row 2: p3, (k3, p3) to end of row.

Rows 3 and 4: rep last two rows once more.

Row 5: p3, (k3, p3) to end of row.

Row 6: k3 (p3, k3) to end of row.

Rows 7–8: rep last 2 rows once more.

Rep last 8 rows for pattern.

Double basket stitch

A mixture of vertical and horizontal ribs creates a woven look.

Cast on a multiple of 10 sts, plus 5.

Row 1 (RS): (k1, p1) twice, *k7, p1, k1, p1; rep from * to last st, k1.

Row 2: p1, (k1, p1) twice, *k5, (p1, k1) twice, p1; rep from * to end.

Rows 3–4: rep last 2 rows once more.

Row 5: k6, *p1, k1, p1, k7; rep from * to last 9 sts, p1, k1, p1, k6.

Row 6: *k5, (p1, k1) twice, p1; rep from * to last 5 sts, k5.

Rows 7–8: rep last 2 rows once more.

Rep last 8 rows for pattern.

Woven stitch

A mixture of a 2 x 2 rib and stockinette stitch produces a fabric that looks as if it is made up of many woven strips.

Cast on a multiple of 4 sts, plus 2.

Row 1 (RS): knit.

Row 2: purl.

Row 3: k2, (p2, k2) to end of row.

Row 4: p2, (k2, p2) to end of row.

Row 5: knit.

Row 6: purl.

Row 7: p2, (k2, p2) to end of row.

Row 8: k2, (p2, k2) to end of row.

Rep last 8 rows for pattern.

Wheat ear

A broken rib that looks like fields of corn.

Cast on an odd number of sts.

Row 1 (RS): k1 (p1, k1) to end of row.

Row 2: p1 (k1, p1) to end of row.

Rep last 2 rows twice more.

Row 7: p1 (k1, p1) to end of row.

Row 8: k1 (p1, k1) to end of row.

Rep last 2 rows twice more.

Rep last 12 rows for pattern.

Ladders

A mixture of rib and garter stitch.

Cast on a multiple of 6 sts, plus 4.

Row 1 (RS): knit.

Row 2: p4, (k2, p4) to end of row.

Row 3: knit.

Row 4: p1, k2, (p4, k2) to last st, p1.

Rep last 4 rows for pattern.

Ribbed diagonals

A rib moved along each row to create textured diagonal lines.

Cast on a multiple of 8 sts.

Row 1 (RS): (k4, p4) to end of row.
Row 2: (k3, p4, k1) to end of row.
Row 3: (p2, k4, p2) to end of row.
Row 4: (k1, p4, k3) to end of row.
Row 5: (p4, k4) to end of row.
Row 6: (p3, k4, p1) to end of row.
Row 7: (k2, p4, k2) to end of row.
Row 8: (p1, k4, p3) to end of row.
Rep last 8 rows for pattern.

Knit and purl diamonds

These little raised diamonds are caused by placing purl stitches onto stockinette.

Cast on a multiple of 8 sts, plus 1.

Row 1 (RS): k4, (p1, k7) to end of row.
Row 2: p3, (k1, p1, k1, p5) to last 6 sts, k1, p1, k1, p3.
Row 3: k2, (p1, k3) to last 3 sts, p1, k2.
Row 4: p1, (k1, p5, k1, p1) to end of row.
Row 5: (p1, k7) to last st, p1.
Row 6: p1, (k1, p5, k1, p1) to end of row.
Row 7: k2, (p1, k3) to last 3 sts, p1, k2.
Row 8: p3, (k1, p1, k1, p5) to last 6 sts, k1, p1, k1, p3.
Rep last 8 rows for pattern.

Textured chevrons

Knit and purl zigzags.

Cast on a multiple of 8 sts, plus 1.

Row 1: k1, (p7, k1) to end of row.

Row 2: p1, (k7, p1) to end of row.

Row 3: k2, (p5, k3) to last 7 sts, p5, k2.

Row 4: p2, (k5, p3) to last 7 sts, k5, p2.

Row 5: k3, (p3, k5) to last 6 sts, p3, k3.

Row 6: p3, (k3, p5) to last 6 sts, k3, p3.

Row 7: k4, (p1, k7) to last 5 sts, p1, k4.

Row 8: p4, (k1, p7) to last 5 sts, k1, p4.

Row 9: Rep row 2.

Row 10: Rep row 1.

Row 11: Rep row 4.

Row 12: Rep row 3.

Row 13: Rep row 6.

Row 14: Rep row 5.

Row 15: Rep row 8.

Row 16: Rep row 7.

Rep last 16 rows for pattern.

Chevron stripes

Make colorful striped zigzags by working increases and decreases. You can alter the width of the zigzags by adding or subtracting a multiple of two.

With color A, cast on a multiple of 14 sts, plus 2.

Row 1 (WS): purl.

Row 2: k1, inc into next st, k4, sl1, k1, psso, k2tog, k4, *inc into each of next 2 sts, k4, sl1, k1, psso, k2tog, k4; rep from * to last 2 sts, inc into next st, k1.

Change to color B.

Row 3: purl.

Row 4: Rep row 2.

Change to color A.

Rep last 4 rows for pattern.

Garter chevron stripes

The chevron, but with added garter rows for texture.

With color A, cast on a multiple of 14 sts, plus 2.

Row 1 (WS): purl.

Row 2: k1, inc into next st, k4, sl1, k1, psso, k2tog, k4, *inc into each of next 2 sts, k4, sl1, k1, psso, k2tog, k4; rep from * to last 2 sts, inc into next st, k1.

Row 3: purl.

Change to color B.

Row 4: Rep row 2.

Row 5: knit.

Change to color A.

Row 6: knit.

Row 7: purl.

Row 8: Rep row 2.

Rep last 8 rows for pattern.

Pleats

Use a slipped stitch to create perfect folds for crisp pleats in skirts or empire lines. To create a fold line on the right side of stockinette stitch, work a slip stitch on the knit side; for a fold line on the reverse, work a slip stitch on the purl side. A series of these paired folds creates pleats.

Cast on desired number of stitches for pleated fabric; here we are using a multiple of 12 sts plus 7.

Row 1 (RS): k7, (p1, k3 sl1, k7) to end of row.

Row 2: (p11, sl1 pwise) to end of row, p7.

Rep last 2 rows for pattern.

Slipped stitch rib

Work a slipped stitch over a rib—be sure to remember to take your yarn between the front and back when required.

Cast on an odd number of sts.

Row 1 (WS): purl.

Row 2: k1, (yf, sl1 pwise, yb, k1) to end of row.

Rep last 2 rows for pattern.

Fisherman's rib

A very attractive, chunky, and satisfying rib, which is often interchangeable with brioche rib, but made with a slightly different technique.

Cast on an even number of sts.

Row 1: knit.

Row 2: (k1, k1b) across row.

Rep last row for pattern.

Brioche rib

Similar to fisherman's rib but worked differently—remember that here, when knitting two together, you will be knitting a stitch together with its corresponding yarn over.

Cast on an even number of sts.

Row 1: (yo, sl 1, k1) across.

Row 2: (to, sl 1, k2tog) across row.

Rep last row for pattern.

Tweed stitch

A dense, woven-effect fabric, with little stretch. Play around with needle size to vary the drape.

Cast on a multiple of 2 sts, plus 1.

Row 1 (RS): k1, (yf, sl1 pwise, yb, k1) to end of row.

Row 2: p2, (yb, sl1 pwise, yf, p1) to last st, p1.

Rep last 2 rows for pattern.

Tweed stitch (reverse)

The back of tweed stitch is just as nice as the front.

Cast on a multiple of 2 sts, plus 1.

Row 1 (WS): k1, (yf, sl1 pwise, yb, k1) to end of row.

Row 2: p2, (yb, sl1 pwise, yf, p1) to last st, p1.

Rep last 2 rows for pattern.

Dropped stitch

Dropped stitches are formed by wrapping the yarn round more than once when forming the knit stitch, then dropping off all extra loops on the return row. It is a fun and quick-to-knit stitch, and is great for highlighting fancy yarns.

Cast on any number of sts.

Rows 1–3: knit.

Row 4: knit all sts, wrapping yarn around RHN 3 times per stitch instead of once.

Row 5: knit all sts, dropping off extra 2 loops per stitch as you go.

Rows 6–7: knit.

Rep rows 4–7 for pattern.

Twisted dropped stitch

An alternative to dropped stitch, where the elongated stitches are twisted in a very attractive way.

Cast on any number of sts.

Rows 1–3: knit.

Row 4: Insert needle into the stitch as if to knit. Instead of wrapping the yarn around the back needle to create a regular knit stitch, wrap yarn around both needles and then wrap around the back needle. Complete stitch as you would normally.

Rows 5–7: knit.

Rep rows 4–7 for pattern.

Wavy dropped stitch

This is formed in the same way as dropped stitch, except by varying the amount of extra times the yarn is wrapped to create a wavy line.

Cast on a multiple of 10 sts, plus 7.

Rows 1–3: knit.

Row 4: k6, *k1, wrapping 2 times, k1 wrapping 3 times, k1, wrapping 4 times, k1 wrapping 3 times, k1 wrapping 2 times, k5; rep from * to last st, k1.

Row 5: knit all stitches, dropping off all extra loops as you go.

Rows 6–7: knit.

Row 8: k1, k1 wrapping 2 times, k1 wrapping 3 times, k1 wrapping 4 times, k1 wrapping 3 times, k1 wrapping 2 times, *k5, k1 wrapping 2 times, k1 wrapping 3 times, k1 wrapping 4 times, k1 wrapping 3 times, k1 wrapping 2 times; rep from * to last st, k1.

Row 9: knit all stitches, dropping off all extra loops as you go.

Rows 10–11: knit across.

Advanced

These stitches make use of the basics, adding in creative shaping and slipped stitches to create textured patterns.

Vertical seersucker

Create a fabric like woven seersucker by slipping stitches.

Cast on a multiple of 11 sts, plus 5.

Row 1 (RS): k1 *(sl 1, k1) twice, k7, rep from * to last 4 sts, (sl 1, k1) twice.

Row 2: p1 *(sl 1, p1) twice, p7, rep from * to last 4 sts, (sl 1, p1) twice.

Row 3: k2, sl 1, k1, sl 1, *k6, (sl 1, k1) twice, sl 1; rep from * to last 5 sts, (k1, sl 1) twice, k1.

Row 4: p2, sl 1, p1, sl 1, *p6, (sl 1, p1) twice, sl 1; rep from * to last 11 sts, p6, (sl 1, p1) twice, p1.

Rep last 4 rows for pattern.

Horizontal seersucker

Again, like a woven seersucker fabric, but with horizontal stripes.

Cast on any number of sts, using needles 0.5 mm smaller than suggested.

Rows 1–6: knit.

**Change to needles 0.5mm larger than suggested.

Row 7: knit twice into every stitch.

Rows 8–12: work in st st, beg with a p row.

Change back to the fine needles.

Row 13: (k2tog) across row.

Rows 14–18: knit**.

Work between ** and ** for length of fabric.

Trinity stitch

A pretty yet very simple way of creating a bobble-like texture using increases and decreases.

Cast on a multiple of 4 sts.

Row 1 (RS): purl.

Row 2: *(k1, p1, k1) in next st, p3tog; rep from * to end of row.

Row 3: purl.

Row 4: *p3tog, (k1, p1, k1) in next st; rep from * to end of row.

Rep last 4 rows for pattern.

Blackberry stitch

Similar to trinity stitch, but with a lacier look.

Cast on a multiple of 4 sts.

Row 1 (RS): *(k1, yo, k1) all into first st, p3; rep from * to end of row.

Row 2: (p3tog, k3) to end of row.

Row 3: *p3, (k1, yo, k1) all into next st; rep from * to end of row.

Row 4: (k3, p3tog) to end of row.

Rep last 4 rows for pattern.

Crossed dropped stitch

As dropped stitch, but effectively crossing the dropped stitches.

Cast on a multiple of 6 sts.

Rows 1–3: knit.

Row 4: *slip next 6 stitches onto RHN, dropping off extra loops. Insert LHN into first three stitches and pull over next three stitches and onto the LHN needle. Place second three stitches back onto the LHN. Knit all six stitches in the new order onto RHN; rep from*

Knot stitch

Another way of using fast increases and decreases to create texture.

Cast on a multiple of 12 sts, plus 3.

Rows 1–6: work in st st, beg with a k row.

Row 7 (RS): *k9, p3tog, leaving sts on LHN, now knit them together, then purl them together again, and finish stitch, 3sts on RHN; rep from * to end of row.

Rows 8–14: work in st st, beg with a p row.

Row 15: *k3, p3tog, leaving sts on LHN, now knit them together, then purl them together again, and finish stitch, 3sts on RHN; rep from * to end of row.

Rows 16–22: work in st st, beg with a p row.

Rep rows 7–22 for pattern.

Star stitch

A very pretty, spiky pattern using decreases.

Special abbreviation: star = p3tog, leaving all sts on needle, yo, p same sts together again, finishing stitch by removing from needle.

Cast on a multiple of 4 sts, plus 1.

Row 1 (RS): knit.

Row 2: p1 (make star, p1) to end of row.

Row 3: knit.

Row 4: p3, make star, (p1, make star) to last 3 sts, p3.

Rep last 4 rows for pattern.

Two-color star stitch

As star stitch, but work rows 1 and 2 in yarn A and rows 3 and 4 in yarn B throughout.

Fur stitch

A fabulous pile fabric that can be left loopy or cut to create a rug effect.

Cast on any multiple of sts and work a fur stitch row on an RS row as often as you wish depending on desired pile. Work all non-fur rows as a k row.

Fur stitch row (RS): k next st without letting it drop off the LH needle, yfwd, pass yarn around thumb or piece of cardboard to make loop approx 1 in (2 cm) long (or desired length), yb and k into the back of st on LH needle, this time completing it by letting it drop off. Pass 1st loop of the st (now on RH needle) over 2nd loop of st and off the needle to secure st.

Striped seed 1

If it was possible to make seed stitch even prettier, this is how—using two colors and a slip stitch.

Slip all sts pwise.

Cast on an odd number of sts with yarn A.

Row 1 (RS): k1 (sl 1, k1) to end of row.

Row 2: k1, (yfwd, sl 1, yb, k1) to end of row.

Change to yarn B.

Row 3: k2, (sl 1, k1) to last st, k1.

Row 4: k2, (yfwd, sl1, yb, k1) to last st, k1.

Change to yarn A.

Rep last 4 rows for pattern.

Striped seed 2

As striped seed 1, but working alternately in two-row stripes of yarns A, B, and C.

Dotted squares

A variation of the previous stitches, creating an attractive check.

Slip all sts pwise.

Cast on a multiple of 10 sts, plus 9 using yarn A.

Row 1 (RS): knit.

Row 2: purl.

Rows 3–4: Rep rows 1 and 2.

Change to yarn B.

Row 5: k1, sl 1, k1, sl 3, * (k1, sl 1) 3 times, k1, sl 3; rep from * to last 3 sts, k1, sl 1, k1.

Row 6: k1, yfwd, sl1 1, yb, k1, yf, sl 3, yb, *(k1, yfwd, sl 1, yb) 3 times, k1, yfwd, sl 3, yb; rep from * to last 3 sts, k1, yfwd, sl 1, yb, k1.

Change to yarn A.

Row 7: knit.

Row 8: purl.

Rows 9–16: Rep last 4 rows twice more.

Rows 17–18: Rep rows 5 and 6 again.

Rep last 18 rows for pattern.

Vertical stripes

Use slipped stitch to create vertical stripes.

Cast on a multiple of 2 sts, plus 1 using yarn A.

Row 1 (RS): knit.

Row 2: purl.

Change to yarn B.

Row 3: k1, (sl 1, k1) to end of row.

Row 4: p1 (sl 1, p1) to end of row.

Change to yarn A.

Row 5: k2, sl 1, (k1, sl 1) to last 2 sts, k2.

Row 6: p2, sl 1, (p1, sl 1) to last 2 sts, p2.

Rep rows 3–6 for pattern.

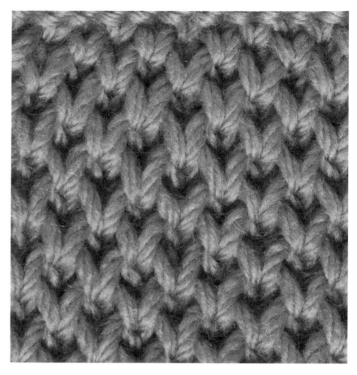

Two-color fisherman's rib

This technique is the same as fisherman's rib, but needs to be knitted using a circular needle or two double-pointed needles, as you sometimes do not turn the work, even though you are working in rows—you simply slide all the stitches to opposite end of the needle when you finish a row when you see the direction "slide."

Cast on a multiple of 2 sts, plus 1, using yarn A.

Row 1: p1, (k1, p1) to end, slide stitches to opposite end of needle. Change to yarn B.

Row 2: p1, (k1b, p1) to end of row, turn work. Change to yarn A.

Row 3: (k1b, p1) to last st, k1b, slide. Change to yarn B.

Row 4: k1 (p1b, k1) to end of row, turn work. Change to yarn A.

Row 5: (p1b, k1) to last st, p1b, slide.

Rep rows 2–5 for pattern.

Fisherman's honeycomb rib

This uses the same technique as fisherman's rib to create an attractive honeycomb effect.

Cast on a multiple of 2 sts.

Row 1 (RS): knit.

Row 2: knit.

Row 3: (k1, k1B) to end of row.

Row 4: *k the next st together with the slipped thread of stitch below on previous row, k1; rep from * to end of row.

Row 5: (k1B, k1) to end of row.

Row 6: *k1, k the next st tog with slipped thread as with row 4; rep from * to end of row.

Rep rows 3–6 for pattern.

Brick stitch

Use slipped stitches to create blocks formed in a brickwork pattern.

Cast on a multiple of 4 sts, plus 1.

Row 1 (RS): k4, *k1 wrapping yarn twice round needle, k3; rep from * to last st, k1.

Row 2: p4, (sl 1 pwise, p3) to last st, p1, (dropping off all extra loops when slipping sts).

Row 3: k4, (sl 1 pwise, k3) to last st, k1.

Row 4: k4, (yfwd, sl 1 pwise, yb, k3) to last st, k1.

Row 5: k2, *k1 wrapping yarn twice round needle, k3; rep from * to last 3sts, k1, wrapping yarn twice round needle, k2.

Row 6: p2, (sl 1 pwise, p3) to last 3 sts, sl 1 pwise, p2, (dropping off all extra loops when slipping sts).

Row 7: k2 (sl 1 pwise, k3) to last 3 sts, sl 1 pwise, k2.

Row 8: k2, (yfwd, sl 1 pwise, yb, k3) to last 3sts, sl 1 pwise, yb, k2.

Rep last 8 rows for pattern.

Slip stitch check 1

Use slip stitch and two colors to create a checkered effect.

Cast on a multiple of 8 sts plus 6, using yarn A.

Rows 1–2: knit.

Change to yarn B.

Row 3: k1, sl 1, k2, sl 1, *k4, sl 1, k2, sl 1; rep from * to last st, k1.

Row 4: p1, sl 1, p2, sl 1, *p4, sl 1, p2, sl 1; rep from * to last st, p1.

Change to yarn A.

Row 5: knit.

Row 6: k1, k next st, wrapping yarn twice, k2, k1 wrapping yarn twice, *k4, k1 wrapping yarn twice, k2, k1 wrapping yarn twice; rep from * to last st, k1.

Change to yarn B.

Row 7: k1, sl 1, k2, sl 1, *k4, sl 1, k2, sl 1; rep from * to last st, k1 (dropping off all extra loops when slipping sts).

Row 8: p1, sl 1, p2, sl 1, *p4, sl 1, p2, sl 1; rep from * to last st, p1.

Row 9: k1, sl 1, k2, sl 1, *k4, sl 1, k2, sl 1; rep from * to last st, k1.

Rep last 2 rows once more.

Row 12: p1, sl 1, p2, sl 1, *p4, sl 1, p2, sl 1; rep from * to last st, p1.

Change to yarn A.

Rep last 12 rows for pattern.

Slip stitch check 2

Using slip stitch and three colors to create a convincing woven-look check.

Cast on a multiple of 6 sts plus 3 with yarn A.

Row 1 (RS): knit.

Change to yarn B.

Row 2: p3, (sl 3 pwise, p3) to end of row.

Row 3: k3, (sl 3 pwise, k3) to end of row.

Rep last 2 rows once more.

Change to yarn A.

Row 6: sl 3 pwise, (p3, sl 3 pwise) to end of row.

Row 7: knit.

Change to yarn C.

Row 8: sl 3 pwise, (p3, sl 3 pwise) to end of row.

Row 9: sl 3 pwise, (k3, sl 3 pwise) to end of row.

Rep last 2 rows once more.

Change to yarn A.

Row 12: p3, (sl 3 pwise, p3) to end of row.

Rep last 12 rows for pattern.

Shell stitch

A very pretty use of dropped stitch techniques.

Cast on a multiple of 6 sts, plus 1.

Row 1: knit.

Row 2: p1, (p5, winding yarn twice rnd needle for each st, p1) to end of row.

Row 3: k1, *sl next 5 sts, dropping all extra sts, pass sts back onto LHN and k all tog, then again pwise, then again kwise, then pwise, then kwise to create 5 sts again, but wrapping yarn twice round needle each time, k1; rep from * to end of row.

Row 4: p1, (k5, dropping off all extra loops, p1) to end of row.

Row 5: knit.

Row 6: p4, (p5, winding yarn twice round needle for each st, p1) to last 3 sts, p3.

Row 7: k3 (k1, work across next 5sts as given for row 3) to last 4 sts, k4.

Row 8: p4, (k5, dropping off all extra loops, p1) to last 3 sts, p3.

Rep last 8 rows for pattern.

Mini bobbles

A cute textured bobbled fabric using increases and decreases.

Special abbreviation: MB = make bobble: (p1, k1, p1, k1) all into next st, pass 2nd, 3rd, 4th sts all over 1st st.

Cast on a multiple of 2 sts, plus 1.

Row 1 (RS): knit.
Row 2: k1 (MB, k1) to end of row.
Row 3: knit.
Row 4: k2 (MB, k1) to last st, k1.

Rep last 4 rows for pattern.

Diagonal stockinette stitch

Stockinette stitch on the bias to create an interesting stitch.

Cast on any number of sts.

Row 1: purl.
Row 2: *cross 1 st to the right by passing needle in front of 1st st on LHN and knitting the next st, without finishing the st, now knit 1st st and drop both sts from needle tog; rep from * to end of row.
Row 3: p1, *cross 1 st to right in same way as row 2, but this time purling the stitches when crossing; rep from * to last st, p1.

Rep rows 2–3 for pattern.

Mini bobbles—two-color

Work as mini bobbles, but work rows 1 and 2 in yarn A and rows 3 and 4 in yarn B.

Smocking stitch

This stitch produces a look similar to a smocked fabric.

Cast on a multiple of four sts, plus 2.

Row 1: *k1, yfwd, sl 3 pwise, with yarn in front of 3 sl sts, wrap round RHN once; rep from * to last 2 sts, k2.

Row 2: purl all sts, letting all extra loops drop to RS of work.

Row 3: knit.

Row 4: purl.

Row 5: k, * with RHN, pick up long thread and ktog with next st, yfwd, sl 3, with yarn in front of 3 sl sts, wrap round RHN once; rep from * to last 4sts, with RHN, pick up long thread and knit tog with next st, k3.

Row 6: purl all sts, letting all extra loops drop to back of work.

Row 7: knit.

Row 8: purl.

Rep last 8 rows for pattern.

Woven basket stitch 1

A stitch to create a woven look to your knitting.

Cast on an even number of sts.

Row 1 (RS): K2tog tbl, dropping only the first loop off left-hand needle, * k rem st on left-hand needle tog with next st along on left- hand needle tbl, again dropping only the first loop off left-hand needle; rep from * until 1 loop rems on left-hand needle, k1 tbl.

Row 2: P2tog, dropping only the first loop off left-hand needle, * p rem st on left-hand needle tog with next st along on left-hand needle, again dropping only the first loop off left-hand needle; rep from * until 1 loop rems on left-hand needle, p1.

Rep last 2 rows for pattern.

Woven basket stitch 2

An alternative but just as attractive looking woven style stitch.

Cast on a multiple of 2 sts.

Row 1: *pass RHN behind first st, k next st, then k first st in normal way; rep from * to end of row.

Row 2: p1, (p 2nd st, then p 1st st) to last st, p1.

Rep last 2 rows for pattern.

Lace stitches

Advanced stitches using lace for an attractive finish.

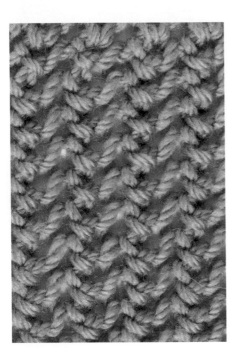

Simple eyelet lace (faggot lace)

The simplest form of lace, using an allover eyelet hole to create an open mesh fabric.

Cast on an odd number of stitches.

Row 1: knit.

Row 2: k1, (yo, k2tog) across row.

Rep row 2 for pattern. Before you bind off, work row 1 once more.

Diagonal eyelet lace

A variation on eyelet lace.

Cast on an odd number of stitches.

Row 1: knit.

Row 2: k1, (yo, k2tog) across row.

Row 3: knit.

Row 4: k2, (yo, k2tog) to last st, k1.

Rep last 2 rows for pattern, ending with a row 1.

Simple eyelet lace variation

This variation makes the eyelets more pronounced.

Cast on an odd number of stitches.

Row 1: knit.

Row 2: k1, (yo, k2tog) across row.

Rep last 2 rows for pattern, ending with a row 1.

Faggoting ribs

Using the faggoting eyelet stitch in panels for an attractive rib.

Cast on a multiple of 4 sts, plus 2.

Row 1: k3, (yo, sl1, k1, psso, k2) to last 3 sts, yo, sl1, k1, psso, k1.

Row 2: p3, (yo, p2tog, p2) to last 3 sts, yo, p2tog, p1.

Rep last 2 rows for pattern.

Dotted eyelet stitch

A pretty use of the simple eyelet holes to create a dotted fabric.

Cast on a multiple of 4 sts, plus 3.

Row 1: knit.

Row 2: purl.

Row 3: (k2, ktog, yo) to last three sts, k3.

Row 4: purl.

Row 5: knit.

Row 6: purl.

Row 7: (k2tog, yo, k2) to last 3 sts, k2tog, yo, k1.

Row 8: purl.

Rep last 8 rows for pattern.

Eyelet chevron

Using eyelets as an increase in a chevron gives a pretty effect, perfect for threading ribbons through.

Cast on a multiple of 14 sts plus 2 with yarn A.

Row 1: purl.

Row 2: k1,*k1, yo, k4, sl1, k1, psso, k2tog, k4, yo, k1*, repeat from to last st, K1.

Rep last 2 rows for pattern, changing color every 4 rows and ending with a row 1.

Lace chevron

An attractive zigzag pattern produced by working eyelets.

Cast on a multiple of 10 sts, plus 1.

Row 1 (and every odd row): purl.

Row 2: (k5, yo, ssk, k3) to last st, k1.

Row 4: (k3, k2tog, yo, k1, yo, ssk, k2) to last st, k1.

Row 6: (k2, k2tog, yo, k3, yo, ssk, k1) to last st, k1.

Row 8: (k1, k2tog, yo, k5, yo, ssk) to last st, k1.

Row 10: k2tog, yo, k7, *yo, sl1, k2tog, psso, yo, k7; rep from * to last 2 sts, yo, ssk.

Rep last 10 rows for pattern.

Lacy ribs

Mixing rib and lace.

Row 1 (WS): (p2, k1) to last 2 sts, p2.

Row 2: (k2, p1, yo, ssk, p1) to last 2 sts, k2.

Row 3: rep row 1.

Row 4: (k2, p1, k2tog, yo, p1) to last 2 sts, p2.

Rep last 4 rows for pattern.

Feather and fan stitch

A soft, wavelike pattern that can be worked over garter or stockinette stitch.

Cast on a multiple of 18 sts, plus 2. (Bottom/Cast on edge of stitch is to the right hand side of the above picture).

Row 1: knit.

Row 2: purl.

Row 3: k1 *[k2tog] 3 times, [yo, k1] 6 times [k2tog] 3 times; rep from * to last st k1.

Row 4: knit.

Rep last 4 rows for pattern.

Striped feather and fan

As feather and fan, but work four-row stripes alternately of two colors throughout. (Bottom/Cast on edge of stitch is to the right hand side of the above picture).

Diamond eyelets

Pretty clusters of eyelet holes.

Pattern text Cast on a multiple of 8 sts.

Row 1 (and every other row): purl.

Row 2: knit.

Row 4: k4, (yo, ssk, k6) to last 4 sts, k4.

Row 6: k1, (k2tog, yo, k1, yo, ssk, k3) to last 2 sts, k2.

Row 8: rep row 4.

Row 10: knit.

Row 12: k7, (yo, ssk, k6) to last st, k1.

Row 14: k5, (k2tog, yo, k1, yo, ssk, k3) to last 3 sts, k3.

Row 16: rep row 12.

Rep last 16 rows for pattern.

Diamond leaves

A stunning, geometric, yet seemingly organic stitch.

Cast on a multiple of 10 sts, plus 1.

Row 1 (RS): k3, *k2tog, yo, k1, yo, sl1, k1, psso, k5; rep from * to last 8 sts, k2tog, yo, k1, yo, sl1, k1, psso, k3.

Row 2 (and every other row): purl.

Row 3: k2, *k2tog, (k1, yo) twice, k1, sl1, k1, psso, k3; rep from * to last 9 sts, k2tog, (k1, yo) twice, k1, sl1, k1, psso, k2.

Row 5: k1, *k2tog, k2, yo, k1, yo, k2, sl1, k1, psso, k1; rep from * to end of row.

Row 7: k2tog, *k3, yo, k1, yo, k3, sl1, k2tog, psso; rep from * to last 9 sts, k3, yo, k1, yo, k3, sl1, k1, psso.

Row 9: k1, *yo, sl1, k1, psso, k5, k2tog, yo, k1; rep from * to end of row.

Row 11: k1, *yo, k1, sl1, k1, psso, k3, k2tog, k1, yo, k1; rep from * to end of row.

Row 13: k1, *yo, k2, sl1, k1, psso, k1, k2tog, k2, yo, k1; rep from * to end of row.

Row 15: k1, *yo, k3, sl1, k2tog, psso, k3, yo, k1; rep from * to end of row.

Row 16: purl.

Rep last 16 rows for pattern.

Lace panels

This pattern can be worked as a single panel running the length of a piece of fabric, or all over by repeating across the fabric.

Cast on a multiple of 7 sts, plus 2.

Row 1 (RS): p2, (k5, p2) to end of row.

Row 2: k2, (p5, k2) to end of row.

Row 3: p2, * k2tog, yo, k1, yo, sl1, k1, psso, p2; rep from * to end of row.

Row 4: rep row 2.

Rep last 4 rows for pattern.

Lace wheatsheaves

The alternating placement of the lace holes adds interest to this pretty pattern.

Cast on a multiple of 6 sts, plus 1.

Row 1: (k1, k2tog, yo, k1, yo, sl1, k1, psso) to last st, k1.

Row 2: purl.

Rep last 2 rows 5 more times.

Row 13: (k1, yo, sl1, k1, psso, k1, k2tog, yo) to last st, k1.

Row 14: purl.

Rep last 2 rows 5 more times.

Rep last 24 rows for pattern.

Trellis lace

The shaping direction adds a criss-cross texture to the lace pattern.

Cast on a multiple of 6 sts, plus 5.

Row 1 (RS): k4, (yo, sl1, k2tog, psso, yo, k3) to last st, k1.

Row 2: purl.

Row 3: k1 (yo, sl1, k2tog, psso, yo, k3) to last 4 sts, yo, sl1, k2tog, psso, yo, k1.

Row 4: purl.

Rep last 4 rows for pattern.

Cable stitches

The first 12 cables can be worked as a panel, with reverse stockinette stitch ground, or with two purl stitches either side within stockinette stitch, or as an allover cable pattern, repeated across the fabric with purl stitches between each cable panel.

Six-stitch S-twist cable

A cable that is always held to the front when twisted, to create a rope-style cable that leans to the left.

Each cable worked over 6 sts.

Row 1(RS): k6.

Row 2: p6.

Rep last 2 rows once more.

Row 5: C6F.

Row 6: p6.

Rep last 6 rows for pattern.

Small cable

A cute twisted cable. You can also work the twist the other way, substituting the C4B for C4F.

Each cable worked over 4 sts.

Row 1 (RS): k4.

Row 2: p4.

Row 3: C4B.

Row 4: p4.

Rep last 4 rows for pattern.

Six-stitch Z-twist cable

A cable that is always held to the back when twisted, to create a rope-style cable that leans to the right.

Each cable worked over 6 sts.

Row 1 (RS): k6.

Row 2: p6.

Rep last 2 rows once more.

Row 5: C6B.

Row 6: p6.

Rep last 6 rows for pattern.

Six-stitch "snake" cable

A cable that alternates between holding the stitches at the back and front, to create a cable that lies on top of the work and "snakes" from side to side.

Each cable worked over 6 sts.

Row 1 (RS): k6.

Row 2: p6.

Rep last 2 rows once more.

Row 5: C6B.

Row 6: p6.

Row 7: k6.

Row 8: p6.

Rep last 2 rows once more.

Row 11: C6F.

Row 12: p6.

Rep last 12 rows for pattern.

Long cable
Playing with the number of plain stockinette stitch rows between each twist adds interest to the cable panels.

Each cable worked over 6 sts.

Row 1 (RS): k6.
Row 2: p6.
Row 3: C6B.
Row 4: p6.
Rows 5–8: rep rows 1 and 2.
Row 9: C6B.
Row 10: p6.
Rows 11–18: Rep rows 1 and 2 4 more times.
Rep rows 3–18 for pattern.

Stag horn
A symmetrical cable panel, which you can easily split into two separate cables if you wish.

Cable panel worked over 19 sts.

Row 1 (RS): k8, p3, k8.
Row 2 (and every other row): p8, k3, p8.
Row 3: k4, C4B, p3, C4F, k4.
Row 5: k2, C4B, k2, p3, k2, C4F, k2.
Row 7: C4B, k4, p3, k4, C4F.
Row 8: p8, k3, p8.
Rep rows 3–8 for pattern.

Double cable
Two cables placed symmetrically next to each other to create an attractive braid.

Each cable worked over 12 sts.

Row 1 (RS): k12.
Row 2: p12.
Rep last 2 rows once more.
Row 5: C6B, C6F.
Row 6: p12.
Rep last 6 rows for pattern.

Fishtail cable

This cable is not like a regular cable, which is worked over an even number of stitches. It uses a cable three right (C3R = next 2 sts onto cn and hold at back, k1, then k2 from cn) and cable three left (C3L = next st onto cn and hold at front, k2, then k1 from cn).

Fishtail worked over 7 sts.

Row 1 (RS): k7.

Row 2: p7.

Rep last 2 rows once more.

Row 5: C3L, k1, C3R.

Row 6: p7.

Rep last 6 rows for pattern.

The claw

Similar to the fishtail, but with cable twists worked in the opposite way.

Claw worked over 6 sts.

Row 1 (RS): k6.

Row 2: p6.

Row 3: C3R, C3L.

Row 4: p6.

Rep last 4 rows for pattern.

Braided cable

This cable looks very much like braided hair.

Cable worked over 6 sts.

Row 1 (RS): knit.

Row 2: purl.

Row 3: k2, C4F.

Row 4: purl.

Row 5: C4B, k2.

Row 6: purl.

Rep last 4 rows for pattern.

Diamond cable

A "traveling" cable, which creates a wide diamond pattern, using a double seed-stitch texture within the center to great effect. This cable uses twisted stitches, which are like cables, but using a mixture of knits and purls.

Special abbreviation: T3B = twist 3 back = slip next st onto a cn at back of work, k2, then p1 from cable needle.

T3F = twist 3 back = slip next 2 sts onto a cn at front of work, p1, k2 from cable needle.

Cable panel worked over 13 sts.

Row 1: T3B, (k1, p1) 3 times, k1, T3F.

Row 2: p2, (k1, p1) 4 times, k1, p2.

Row 3: T3F, p1, k1) 3 times, p1, T3B.

Row 4: k1, p2, (k1, p1) 4 times, p1, k1.

Row 5: p1, T3F, (p1, k1) twice, p1, T3B, p1.

Row 6: k2, p2, (k1, p1) 3 times, p1, k2.

Row 7: p2, T3F, p1, k1, p1, T3B, p2.

Row 8: k3, p2, k1, p1, k1, p2, k3.

Row 9: p3, T3F, p1, T3B, p3.

Row 10: k4, p2, k1, p2, k4.

Row 11: p4, C5B, p4.

Row 12: rep row 10.

Row 13: p3, T3B, k1, T3F, p3.

Row 14: rep row 8.

Row 15: p2, T3B, k1, p1, k1, T3F, p2.

Row 16: rep row 6.

Row 17: p1, T3B, (k1, p1) twice, k1, T3F, p1.

Row 18: rep row 4.

Rep last 18 rows for pattern.

Waves and bobbles

When working Aran patterns, bobbles are a commonly used technique.

Special abbreviation: MB = make bobble by working into the front, back and then front again of the next stitch, [turn and knit these 3 sts] 3 times, turn and then sl 1, k2tog, psso to complete the bobble.

Cables worked over 26 sts.

Row 1 (RS): p2, T3B, p5, C6B, p5, T3F, p2.

Row 2: k2, p2, k6, p6, k6, p2, k2.

Row 3: p1, T3B, p4, T5B, T5F, p4, T3F, p1.

Row 4: k1, p2, k5, p3, k4, p3, k5, p2, k1.

Row 5: T3B, p3, T5B, p4, T5F, p3, T3F.

Row 6: p2, k1, MB, k2, p3, k8, p3, k2, MB, k1, p2.

Row 7: T3F, p3, k3, p8, k3, p3, T3B.

Row 8: k1, p2, k3, p3, k8, p3, k3, p2, k1.

Row 9: p1, T3F, p2, T5F, p4, T5B, p2, T3B, p1.

Row 10: k2, p2, [k4, p3] twice, k4, p2, k2.

Row 11: p2, T3F, p3, T5F, T5B, p3, T3B, p2.

Row 12: k1, MB, k1, p2, k5, p6, k5, p2, k1, MB, k1.

Rep last 12 rows for pattern.

Broken cables

An allover cable pattern using double-twisted, short cables.

Cast on a multiple of 8 sts, plus 4.

Row 1 (RS): k4, (p4, k4) to end of row.

Row 2: p4, (k4, p4) to end of row.

Row 3: C4F, (p4, C4F) to end of row.

Row 4: p4, (k4, p4) to end of row.

Rows 5–7: rep rows 1–3.

Row 8: p4, (k4, p4) to end of row.

Row 9: k4, (p4, k4) to end of row.

Row 10: k4, (p4, k4) to end of row.

Row 11: p4, (k4, p4) to end of row.

Row 12: k4, (p4, k4) to end of row.

Row 13: p4 (C4B, p4) to end of row.

Rows 14–17: rep rows 10–13.

Row 18: k4, (p4, k4) to end of row.

Row 19: p4, (k4, p4) to end of row.

Row 20: p4, (k4, p4) to end of row.

Rep last 20 rows for pattern.

Honeycomb

This cable can work as a panel using eight stitches, but looks simply stunning worked all over.

Cast on a multiple of 8 sts, plus 4.

Row 1 (RS): p2, (C4B, C4F) rep from * to last 2 sts, p2.

Row 2 (and every other row): k2, p to last 2 sts, k2.

Row 3: p2, k to last 2 sts, p2.

Row 5: p2, (C4F, C4B) to last 2 sts, p2.

Row 7: rep row 3.

Row 8: k2, p to last 2 sts, k2.

Rep last 8 rows for pattern.

Noughts and crosses

A cable with interlinked crosses and circles for a distinctive pattern.

Cable worked over 8 sts.

Row 1 (RS): knit.

Row 2 (and every other row): purl.

Row 3: C4B, C4F.

Row 5: knit.

Row 7: C4B, C4F.

Row 9: knit.

Row 11: C4F, C4B.

Row 13: knit.

Row 15: C4F, C4B.

Row 16: purl.

Rep last 16 rows for pattern.

Edgings/hems

Creating a decorative edge or hem can complete a
knitted product and make it look far more professional.
Try some of these out for size.

Simple hem

There is a very simple trick for ensuring that your folded-up hem
is neat and crisp; simply add a purl row into stockinette stitch
and the hem will fold naturally along the line.

Cast on the amount of sts required for hem.

Work 8 rows st st, beg with a k row (or desired even number of rows
for depth of hem).

Row 9: purl.

Work 8 rows st st, beg with a p row (or same number of rows as
worked before hemline purl row).

When garment is complete, fold hem along purl hemline and sew
neatly to attach.

Picot hem

Using the same principle as the simple hem, this hem is again
turned back and stitched down later, but uses a row of eyelets to
create a very pretty edging.

Cast on an odd number of sts.

Work 8 rows st st, beg with a k row (or desired even number of rows
for depth of hem).

Row 9: k1 (yo, ktog) to end of row.

Work 8 rows st st, beg with a p row (or same number of rows as
worked before eyelet row).

When garment is complete, fold hem along eyelet hemline and sew
neatly to attach.

Fur fringing

Using a single or double row of fur stitch, you can create either a fringed edge or a hem with ease.

Cast on any number of sts.

Row 1: knit.

Row 2 (RS): *k next st without letting it drop off the LH needle, yfwd, pass yarn around thumb or piece of cardboard to make loop approx ¾ in (2cm) long (or desired length), yb and k into the back of st on LH needle, this time completing it by letting it drop off. Pass 1st loop of the st (now on right hand needle) over 2nd loop of st and off the needle to secure st; rep from * across row.

Row 3: knit.

Now either bind off for an edging, or continue in pattern if you are working the fringe as a hem.

Feather and fan edging

A pretty edging equivalent of the lace feather and fan stitch.

Cast on a multiple of 18 sts, plus 2.

Row 1: knit.

Row 2: purl.

Row 3: k1 *[k2tog] 3 times, [yo, k1] 6 times [k2tog] 3 times; rep from * to last st k1.

Row 4: knit.

Rows 5–10: rep rows 1–4 once more, then rows 1 and 2 again.

Row 11: k1, *k2tog, k5 (k2tog) twice, k5, k2tog; rep from * to last st, k1.

Bind off all sts.

Scalloped edging

A very simple and pretty edging that binds off certain stitches across one row and then casts them on again, as with the buttonhole technique (see page 68).

Cast on a multiple of 7 sts, plus 2.

Row 1: k2, (bind off 5 sts, k2) to end of row.

Row 2: k2, (cast on 5 sts, k2) to end of row.

Row 3: knit.

Row 4: knit.

Now either bind off for an edge or continue in pattern for a hem.

Leaf edging

This edging is knit sideways rather than lengthwise so that you can simply continue knitting until the desired length is reached. Cast on 8 sts.

Row 1 (RS): k5, yo, k1, yo, k2. 10 sts.
Row 2: p6, inc 1k, k3. 11 sts.
Row 3: k4, p1, k2, yo, k1, yo, k3. 13 sts.
Row 4: p8, inc 1k, k4. 14 sts.
Row 5: k4, p2, k3, yo, k1, yo, k4. 16 sts.
Row 6: p10, inc 1k, k5. 17 sts.
Row 7: k4, p3, k4, yo, k1, yo, k5. 19 sts.
Row 8: p12, inc 1k, k6. 20 sts.
Row 9: k4, p4, yb, skpo, k7, k2tog, k1. 18 sts.
Row 10: p10, inc 1k, k7. 19 sts.
Row 11: k4, p5, yb, skpo, k5, k2tog, k1. 17 sts.
Row 12: p8, inc 1k, k2, p1, k5. 18 sts.
Row 13: k4, p1, k1, p4, yb, skpo, k3, k2tog, k1. 16 sts.
Row 14: p6, inc 1k, k3, p1, k5. 17 sts.
Row 15: k4, p1, k1, p5, yb, skpo, k1, k2tog, k1. 15 sts.
Row 16: p4, inc 1k, k4, p1, k5. 16 sts.
Row 17: k4, p1, k1, p6, yb, sl 1, k2tog, psso, k1. 14 sts.
Row 18: p2tog, cast off 5 sts using p2tog as the first of these sts (1 st on RHN), k1, p1, k5. 8 sts.

Rep last 18 rows for pattern.

Bell edging

A beautiful edge which gives a ruffled hem.

Cast on a multiple of 12 sts, plus 3.

Row 1: p3, (k9, p3) to end of row.
Row 2: k3, (p9, k3) to end of row.
Row 3: p3, (ssk, k5, k2tog, p3) to end of row.
Row 4: k3, (p7 k3) to end of row.
Row 5: p3, (ssk, k3, k2tog, p3) to end of row.
Row 6: k3, (p5, k3) to end of row.
Row 7: p3, (ssk, k1, k2tog, p3) to end of row.
Row 8: k3, (p3, k3) to end of row.
Row 9: p3, (sl2tog, k1, psso, p3) to end of row.
Row 10: k3, (p1, k3) to end of row.
Row 11: p3, (k1, p3) to end of row.
Row 12: Rep row 10.

Picot bind off

A fabulously pretty edging for a bound-off edge/neckline.

Work on a multiple of 3 sts, plus 2, until you are ready to bind off.

Bind off two stitches, one stitch on the right needle.

*Slip this stitch back to the left-hand needle, cast on 2 sts, bind off 4 sts; rep from * to end of row.

Fasten off yarn.

I-cord

An I-cord is a great, quick and simple way to make a cord, or tube of knitting, using two double pointed needles. Use the cord as a button loop, a drawstring, or as an embellishment.

Cast on any amount of sts, but a small number will create the neatest, closed cord. 3 to 5 is perfect. Work quite tightly, with needles slightly smaller than suggested.

Using 2 double pointed needles, cast on set number of sts and k 1 row.

Instead of turning a row, slide sts to opposite end of the needle, and passing yarn from left of work to right, knit another row to roll sts into a tube.

Continue in this way for every foll row.

Fasten off yarn.

Suppliers

Artesano LTD
www.artesanoyarns.co.uk
Unit G, Lamb's Farm Business
Park
Basingstoke Rd
Swallowfield
Reading, Berkshire
RG7 1PQ, UK
+44 (0)118 9503350

Berroco, Inc
http://berroco.com/
1 Tupperware Drive
Suite 4
N. Smithfield, RI 02896

Blue Sky Alpacas
http://blueskyalpacas.com/
PO Box 88
Cedar, MN 55011
763–753–5815

Brown Sheep Company, Inc.
http://brownsheep.com
100662 County Road 16
Mitchell, Nebraska 69357
1–800–826–9136

Cascade Yarns
http://www.cascadeyarns.com/

Classic Elite Yarns
http://wwwclassiceliteyarns.com
122 Western Avenue
Lowell, MA 01851
978–453–2837

Coats PLC
Coats.com
3430 Toringdon Way, # 301
Charlotte, NC 28277
1–800–242–8095

Colinette Yarns LTD
http://www.colinette.com/
Banwy workshops
Llanfair Caereinion, Powys
SY210SG
01938 810128

Debbie Bliss
http://www.debbieblissonline.com

Designer Yarns
http://www.designeryarns.uk.com/
Unit 8–10 Newbridge Industrial
Estate
Pitt Street, Keighley
West Yorkshire, BD21 4PQ
+44 (0)1535 664222

J C Rennie & Co. LTD
www.jcrennie.com
Milladen
Mintlaw, Scotland
AB42 8LA
+44 (0)1779 871400
info@jcrennie.com

Juno Fibre Arts
www.etsy.com/shop/JunoFibreArts

King Cole
http://www.kingcole.co.uk/
Merrie Mills
Elliott Street
Silsden, Keighley
West Yorkshire
BD20 0DE
01535 650230

Lion Brand Yarn
http://cache.lionbrand.com/
135 Kero Road
Carlstadt, NJ 07072
800–258–9276

Lornas Laces
www.lornaslaces.net
4229 North Honore St
Chicago, IL 60613
USA
773–935–3803

Louet
www.louet.com/
3425 Hands Rd,
Prescott, ON, Canada
K0E 1T0
613–925–4502

Madeleine Tosh
http://madelinetosh.com
7515 Benbrook Pkwy
Benbrook TX 76126
817.249.3066

Malabrigo Yarn
http://www.malabrigoyarn.com/
786 866 6187

Orkney Angora
www.orkneyangora.co.uk/
+ 44 1857 600421

Quince & Co
www.quinceandco.com
877–309–6762

Red Heart Yarn
http://www.redheart.com/

Rowan Yarns
http://www.knitrowan.com/

Sirdar Spinning LTD
www.sirdar.co.uk
Flanshaw Lane
Wakefield
West Yorkshire
WF2 9ND
+44 (0)1924 371 501

Sweet Georgia
www.sweetgeorgiayarns.com
#401–228 East 4th Avenue
Vancouver, BC V5T 1G5
Canada
(604) 569–6811

Tunney Wool Company
915 N 28th St.
Philadelphia, PA 19130
888–673–0260

Picture credits

All other images are the copyright of Quintet Publishing Ltd. While every effort has been made to credit contributors, Quintet Publishing would like to apologize should there have been any omissions or errors—and would be pleased to make the appropriate corrections for future editions of the book.

A = above, B = below, L = left, R = right, C = center, T = top, F = far

Alamy 7 © V&A Images; 11T © Bert Folsom; 11B © MISCELLANEOUSTOCK; 12 © Phil Degginger; 75BR © studiomode.

Getty Images 20 © Brian Hagiwara; 25C © Steve Gorton; 38TL © Kristin Duvall; 60TL © Johner.

iStock 15L, 15BL, 32.

Mary Evans 9 © Mary Evans Picture Library/LESLEY BRADSHAW.

Picture Desk 8T, 8B.

Shutterstock 10T, 10BL, 10BCL, 10BCR, 10BR, 14, 17, 18B, 22T, 24T, 27C, 27BR, 28, 30, 31TR, 51TL, 70BL, 71TR, 72, 74, 75BL, 76, 77.

Quintet Publishing would like to thank the models:
Clemintine Anicet, Kerstin Heigl, Natasha Kate, Duncan Maïs, Yusuf Charles, and Kyla Lewis.

Index